DATE DUE JUN 0 6

GAYLORD			PRINTED IN U.S.A.

UFFIZI
FLORENCE

UFFIZI
FLORENCE

Newsweek/GREAT MUSEUMS OF THE WORLD

NEW YORK, N.Y.

**GREAT MUSEUMS
OF THE WORLD**

Editorial Director—Carlo Ludovico Ragghianti
Assistant—Giuliana Nannicini
Translation and Editing—Editors of ARTNEWS

UFFIZI FLORENCE

Texts by:

Gigetta Dalli Regoli

Giorgio Faggin

Gian Lorenzo Mellini

Raffaele Monti

Anna Pallucchini

Design:

Fiorenzo Giorgi

Published by

NEWSWEEK, INC.
& ARNOLDO MONDADORI EDITORE

1st Printing 1968
2nd Printing 1972
3rd Printing 1973
4th Printing 1974
5th Printing 1979

ISBN: Clothbound Edition 0-88225-238-0
ISBN: Deluxe Edition 0-88225-213-5

Library of Congress Catalog Card No. 69-18514

INTRODUCTION

LUISA BECHERUCCI
Director, Uffizi Gallery

The Uffizi Gallery today has a special position among Italian museums, not only because of the exceptional quality of its possessions, but also because of the fascinating topicality of its problems. For four centuries, since its creation by the Medici, who had become the sovereigns of Tuscany, the Uffizi has held a position in the forefront of world culture. Today, however, assiduous efforts are required to maintain this primacy and ensure its continuation in the future. We are on a dividing line between the present social and cultural system, which is being brusquely and even violently challenged, and a new one that is dawning in the midst of tumultuous but still vague demands. Even the museums, especially the great ones, like the Uffizi, with the experience of centuries behind them, cannot ignore these developments. It is in the character of the Uffizi Gallery, however, to adjust to circumstances, for it has never been a static institution of unchanging beauty like, for instance, the splendid Galleria Palatina of the Pitti Palace, which has remained an intact 17th-century picture gallery. The Uffizi, on the other hand, has always evolved in response to the needs of a culture in which it has from the beginning played an essential part. Today, to remain true to its mission the Gallery must again, as at every turning point in civilization, make a further effort to adjust to and participate in a new situation. This is its present problem, the exact terms of which have been the object of years of study, as well as of laborious discussion.

The Gallery today appears in the specialized form of a *pinacotheca,* that is, a collection made up principally of works of pictorial art. This collection, however, contains the fundamental works of one of the major phases of civilization, the Renaissance, which achieved its highest expression in art. Concerning the Uffizi paintings, Ragghianti has said that "without them history cannot be written." The statement recognizes that in these basic works, more than in literary and philosophical texts, the Renaissance revealed the new spirit of inquiry, which renewed the conception of the world because it undertook a new, direct experience of nature, as of man, in every aspect of being. The means utilized in acquiring this experience were the means of art. It was not the physical eye but the intellectual eye, aided by the mathematical resources elaborated in the new science of perspective, that was trained on the multiplicity of phenomena to investigate their infinite relationships. And in its affirmation through images of the "incessant becoming" and of "motion which is the cause of all life," perspective was the forerunner on the paths taken by modern science.

At the Uffizi today may be seen the essential stages in this adventure of the mind. Stages that bear the names of Cimabue, Giotto, Duccio and Simone Martini: the first promoters of "natural art." Working in terms of this art, Masaccio, Piero della Francesca, Pollaiolo and Botticelli produced a succession of discoveries, leading to the new dynamic "classicism" of Leonardo, Michelangelo, Raphael and Titian. It also led beyond, in a continual dialectic of acceptance and forward-looking negations, to Rubens, Rembrandt and Caravaggio. In all of this exceptional assembly of great masters we shall consider not their forgotten works debatably brought to notice again by the critics, or the more tired examples of their creative powers, but those certified by the oldest and soundest tradition, and those in which their thought attained their most lucid intuitions. Such paintings as Botticelli's *La Primavera* (Spring), Leonardo's *Adoration of the Magi,* Michelangelo's *Holy Family* or Raphael's *Leo X* have become cultural commonplaces, in history and art, and are almost worn down by centuries of admiration. The main theme they compose at the Uffizi is included, as if in a clarifying commentary, in the thick web of evolution from which the masterpieces emerged, and from which they took their start toward original conclusions. Around the examples of Florentine and Italian art are spread those of every country. The great *Portinari Triptych* by Hugo van der Goes, one of the crucial works in Flemish painting, is placed so that it can be compared with Botticelli; and all of 15th-century Europe is summed up in this juxtaposition. Caravaggio and Rembrandt, the pivotal figures of the 17th century, are shown in the same room with each other. Although the Uffizi's exhibits intentionally go no further than the threshold of the 18th century, they show the root stock finally branching out toward modern art. The collection of self-portraits, which includes the great 19th-century French painters, Ingres, Corot and Delacroix, goes up to Ensor in date, and is awaiting a resumption of acquisitions that will complete it up to the present. But a perusal of the Uffizi's contents, benefiting from the sharpened attention of modern criticism, should discover alongside the main line of the exhibits, a more subtle and complex theme that the radiance, as it were, of the great examples has relegated to the shadows. Once discovered, it will tell us a great deal about the significance of the Gallery and its inmost character.

It reached this last form by degrees, through cultural stages that have not canceled each other out, but have left distinct traces visible to anyone who observes attentively. Their rediscovery will give us a continuous narrative of centuries of events, not only concerning the Uffizi Gallery but also the history and conception of museums.

Going from room to room full of masterpieces, one does not notice that one of the great works is the Gallery itself, with its form modulated in a rhythm of harmonious proportions that have allowed it to be enlarged and altered over the centuries without losing its identity. It is the form that Vasari, before the Gallery was created, gave the building that was later to house it. The structure was intended for the citizens' judiciary, the last residue of Florentine republican government, and the Uffizi ("Offices") building was commissioned by Cosimo I to concentrate this branch of the administration under his direct control, as absolute monarch of Florence. But rather than a centralized, overpowering pile on the site along the Via dei Magistrati, Vasari constructed a rhythmical series of harmoniously disposed façades embracing an esplanade otherwise bordered by the bulk of Palazzo Vecchio, the Loggia dei Lanzi and — on the other side — the porticoes opening on the Arno. Vasari, who was a great and inspired town planner, as well as an artist and writer, also built a skillful architectural link between the medieval city, enclosed within its forbidding stone walls, and the new city which he was laying out beyond the river, on the gently sloping hills around the Pitti Palace then under construction. The fine corridor he built was the elevated "path" that crossed over the Arno toward the new rural outlets. It started from the riverside wing of the Uffizi, above the loggia that was like a critical eye cast by the artist on his own urban creation, which had given Florence a new countenance. With the regular rhythm of its columns, the loggia framed Arnolfo's Tower and Brunelleschi's Dome looming above the ancient roofs, the green slopes of the hills and the course of the river moving off into the broad plain. The city itself, as a work of art, was the first possession of what was to become the Gallery. After Vasari and Cosimo had died, the new Grand Duke, Francesco I, had Bernardo Buontalenti arrange the most precious objects of the Medici collection in rooms above the loggia, associating the beauty of the views with the beauty of these objects. The Tribuna and adjoining rooms, the first constructions intended exclusively for museum purposes, were thus conceived both as housing for the collection and a place for poetic evocation of nature. In form and decoration they gave an active, almost theatrical sense to the beautiful things that filled them. Like actors in the nearby theater which he had constructed on the lower floor of the building, in the Tribuna the objects were made to "perform" under the fanciful direction of Buontalenti. Ancient gems and cameos, silver sculpture by Giambologna alined along the red velvet of the walls next to a few masterpieces of painting, under the vault encrusted with mother of pearl, acted out a complicated allegory: the story of the elements — air, earth, fire, 11 water — subjugated and turned into things of beauty by the mastery of "man the maker." Having passed its zenith at the end of the 16th century, the Renaissance turned to contemplate its past achievements, and in the subtle complexities of Mannerism made them the theme of a charming and fantastic escapism. However, in his *Lives of the Painters, Sculptors and Architects,* Vasari had given the Renaissance its historical consecration, and history, even though still wrapped in legend and allegory, was embodied in the new system that was being created: the Gallery, an organic structure compared to the random assortments of precious or curious things brought together in the medieval treasuries or the curio collections of Northern princes. In the Gallery, man's creations had their own setting to enhance their significance, and were displayed for the visitors' edification as well as for their admiration. It was open to the public, permission to visit being freely granted by the Grand Duke on request. The humanistic view of collections as a means of public education was a continuing factor, and one that Lorenzo the Magnificent had already expressed when he opened the Medici collection of ancient and contemporary art, in the famous garden in the Via Larga, to young artists for study. Among these students had been Leonardo and Michelangelo.

The Uffizi Gallery was the beginning of the first museum, in its modern connotation of a dialogue between art and man. The great encyclopedic systems of the medieval churches, with their complexes of frescoes and rites celebrating a human story with a superhuman ending, were succeeded in the Renaissance gallery by a display whose goal was exclusively knowledge. It is from these premises that the evolution of the modern museum as a means of directly acquiring new experience begins, and from here it starts to refine its methods and increase its specializations. The art museum, the gallery, differentiates itself from the science museum, and aids in the formation of a new discipline: art history.

In this general evolution, from the 17th century to the Enlightenment, the Uffizi maintained its position in the forefront. It was a follower of the new trends, and a friend of Galileo, Cardinal Leopoldo de' Medici, brother of the Grand Duke Ferdinando II, who began the specialized collections of Venetian painting, of drawings, miniatures and artists' self-portraits which on his death became the many different sections of a now enlarged Gallery. Archeological research, which became progressively more systematic in the course of the 18th century, added Etruscan bronzes, urns and vases to the nucleus of classical sculpture, with its outstanding series of Imperial portraits. The Gallery became the universal gathering place of all the components — by now identified by criticism — that make up art and cultural history. It was the great storehouse open to historical investigation, which still maintained the value of a now politically insignificant Florence in the civilization of the world. The last of the Medici, Anna Maria Luisa, wife of the Elector Palatine, was well aware of this when she took steps to avoid the dispersal, after the imminent extinction of her family line, of the collection that had been the greatest glory of her House. She bequeathed it not to the person of the Prince, but to the city of Florence, under the terms of a family agreement with the new sovereign from the House of Lorraine. The words resound with awareness of their own significance: "as an ornament of the State, for the utility of the public and to attract the curiosity of foreigners." These are the circumstances that have ever since nourished the cultural and economic life of Florence.

The intelligent enlightenment of Pietro Leopoldo of Lorraine, who brought from Vienna a sense of the advanced civilization of a great modern capital, infused new life into the Gallery. The Viennese collections were in the midst of being reorganized in accordance with the topographical and chronological criteria current in art history, and this provided the example. The conception of art history as the evolution of phenomena, which Winkelmann had proclaimed for ancient art, found its great exponent in Luigi Lanzi for medieval and modern art. Lanzi's *History of Painting in Italy,* still valid today, which divided the field into schools, provided the lines for his reorganization of the Uffizi Gallery when Pietro Leopoldo entrusted him with the task in 1789. New rooms, in a refined Neo-Classical taste, were opened along the corridors, felicitously taking their place beside the 16th-century rooms, and respecting Vasari's measured harmony. They were the Sala della Niobe and the charming oval Gabinetto delle Gemme. The various Cabinets corresponded to selections of the material, and one of them was devoted to the "Primitives," or the artists who came before the great evolution of 16th-century classicism, and who were beginning to be appreciated again. It is this time that sees the beginning of the specialization in criticism which determines the development of the Gallery in the following century and, one might say, up to today. The more exact classification of the immense amount of material led to the multiplication of the sections, and the need to decentralize them in various locations where they could develop autonomously. While the great collection of Renaissance painting — at the center of art studies between the 19th and 20th centuries — 13 was integrated in the original halls and the Uffizi assumed its definitive character as a picture gallery, whatever was not painting was distributed into separate sections. Sculpture and the minor arts were brought together to form the Bargello Museum; the Etruscan collections, the Museo Archeologico. Later the jewels and prize objects went into the Museo degli Argenti, while the Galleria dell'Accademia was formed from a strict qualitative selection of the paintings, and those by Fra Angelico were collected in the old Convent of San Marco. It was not a dispersal but a proliferation of the great Gallery, which extended itself by means of these sections throughout the city. But the center of Florentine museum life remained the Uffizi, where the Renaissance offered a complete picture of its artistic creativity, which had in the first place created the museum as a tool of knowledge and laid the basis for its evolution in the Gallery itself.

This is what should be shown and explained to today's public at the Uffizi: an unfolding of the complex themes in its historical development. It is a history that today is attracting new people, who are far in time and space from the culture that nevertheless forms the deep substratum of their most forward-looking demands. To bring them closer to it means bringing them closer to themselves and their human reality. This is the task of every modern museum, and also the task of the ancient gallery of Florence. After the great crises of the two World Wars, the relationship between the Uffizi and the public became difficult and seamed with problems. Its present public is made up of ever-increasing masses of visitors from all countries, who are thirsting for knowledge but for the most part deprived of the means of obtaining it. Cloaked in its mantle of age-old prestige, the Gallery was unprepared for this new problem in communication, and was mute before questions that were no longer formulated in the familiar terms.

Today the traditional descriptive labels or printed guides are of no use in explaining a work of art that comes out of a complex cultural background. To use them, a fundamental education is required that the present-day public does not possess. What is needed is the direct explanation, aided by every means of spreading information, from lectures to guided tours and the showing of films on the works that are about to be seen in reality. Although they are difficult to grasp, the attempt must be made to explain these profound creations of mankind. Unless a visit to the Uffizi is made an opportunity to learn something of lasting spiritual value, it will be reduced to a mere means of satisfying curiosity.

This is what modern museums all over the world are now accomplishing, with ever-improving means. They are organizing information systems, which on the one hand are associated with their research programs, and on the other with their didactic activities geared to publicizing the results through energetic public education.

And this is what has determined the Uffizi's present problem, and makes it different from and more complex than those that the other Italian galleries have faced and often resolved. At the Uffizi questions from all over the world have to be answered, and some response must be given to allay the anxieties created by the need to come close to real values. In November 1966, the great disaster brought by the flooding of the Arno was miraculously contained by those most rebellious against every convention of the past, the youth who gave themselves heart and soul to the rescue of art and culture, risking their lives almost as if to find a spiritual anchorage in that past which they felt to be more immediate than the equivocal present. It is this confidence that the Uffizi must nurture again, by every means, bringing its great demonstration of civilization closer to the men of today. The problem is not to disguise or alter an organization whose very form is a form of art, but to make the museum functional, welcoming and comprehensible. The expansion of the Gallery to the entire building of the Uffizi, after the removal of the State Archives which occupy it in part, will provide the space needed for overhauling the organization. Like a novel, a poem or a symphony, the Uffizi has a plot and many themes, and all that is needed is to "reread" its intricacies critically and make them clear to everyone, in order to guide securely an effort that will be of the greatest benefit not only to Florence but to our whole civilization.

Luisa Becherucci

ITALY

Pisan Cross.

Because of its stylistic features, this cross is usually classified as Pisan, like others in Rosano, in S. Frediano and Santo Sepolcro at Pisa. A similar family of crosses painted toward the end of the 12th century exists in the region of Lucca, and its archetype would seem to be the cross in the Cathedral of Sarzana, which was signed by Master Guglielmo in 1138. These monumental crosses, which were conceived as didactic works, derive their distinctive form — the expanded terminal panels — from the Byzantine reliquary crosses that were objects of private devotion. Increased in scale and with the iconography changed, as in this case, from that of the suffering Christ to that of Christ the All-Ruler, they were hung or placed above the iconostasis or the reredos in Romanesque churches, hence the name "stational" crosses. Examples remain in place in a number of churches, and such crosses are also represented in Giotto's frescoes at Assisi.

Tuscany is poor in wall paintings of the 12th century. As the churches did not possess fresco cycles, these historiated crosses were practically their only decoration, which very likely was the reason for their gigantic size. This would also explain the presence of the large panel which derives from the illustrations of the Exultet rolls used in the Easter liturgy, as is shown by the narration, from top to bottom, of the scenes. In a recent restoration, the face of Christ was freed of later redaubings, to reveal its original, stoic aloofness.

CIMABUE. *Madonna and Child in Majesty.*   *p. 20*

Completed a little later than the Assisi frescoes of around 1280 which marked the dramatic peak of the master's imagination, this *Madonna and Child in Majesty* represents the golden maturity of Cimabue, colored by his courtly neo-Carolingian and neo-Byzantine nostalgia. Placed in the same room as the two similar works by Duccio (*page 21*) and Giotto (*page 22*), it does not lose by their presence, but gains in fascination, as the comparison confirms the greatness of the personality of the painter, who must have been the master of the other two artists.

With respect to Giotto's revolutionary humanism, which lay in the future, and Duccio's somewhat later neo-Alexandrian lyricism, Cimabue's *Majesty* remains the greatest among the incunabula of Italian painting. This has been understood since Vasari, who said of Cimabue how marvelous it was that he "should see so much light in the midst of so great darkness." But nowhere on earth is there a better illustration of Dante's idea of a competition between Cimabue and Giotto than in this bringing together of the works of the three masters, though Dante's lines might have been too hasty in their judgment on Cimabue. In this painting Cimabue introduces certain features — apart from the actual expressive means — that will remain constant in Florentine painting, and in the Italian art that follows. These embrace not only the epic serenity of his psychological atmosphere, but also the masculine and forceful aspect of his figures. Compositionally, the work follows a Byzantine scheme, which is however completely transformed. It is interpreted in a fantastically hyperbolic form. The human scale of the

PISAN CROSS
called "CROCE DELL'ACCADEMIA"
End of 12th century
Tempera on panel; 12'4 1/2" × 7'5".
The paint has fallen away from the top of the cross, from a good half of the panel at the right and from the lower left. On the left of the central figure, reading from above: *The Washing of the Feet, The Kiss of Judas, The Flaggelation;* on the right, reading from above: *The Deposition; The Entombment; The Resurrection;* at the feet: *The Way to Calvary;* on the panels of the arms: the *Marys* and *St. John.*
Provenance unknown.

figures below is equated with that of the spectator, and by comparison emphasizes the gigantic, towering proportions of the enthroned Madonna. She seems as tall as a bell tower, and with the human tower formed by the angels creates a space like an immense vessel. This is emphasized by the two perspective vanishing points, above and below, that are linked by the illusion created by the ambiguous form of the throne carried on arches.

CIMABUE
(CENNI DI PEPO)
Florence 1240? — Pisa circa 1302
Madonna and Child in Majesty
Tempera on panel; 12'7 1/2" × 7'3 3/4".
From the High Altar of S. Trinità, Florence

DUCCIO DI BUONINSEGNA
Siena, active from 1278 to 1318
Madonna and Child in Majesty, called the
Rucellai Madonna after the chapel
of the same name in S. Maria Novella,
Florence; it was commissioned by the
Compagnia dei Laudesi in 1285. Tempera
on panel; 14'9" × 9'6". On the frame
there are 30 medallions with busts of saints.

DUCCIO.   *Madonna and Child in Majesty.*

Duccio di Buoninsegna's *Majesty* is dialectically opposed to the Cimabue type, expressing a quite different system of values. Its sweet and idyllic intimacy, however, is set in the same unreal and liturgical context as Cimabue's so that only such a totally complete personality as shown here is able to break through. The extraordinary fact is that Cimabue himself was fascinated by this invention and sought to adopt it in his late Pisan *Majesty,* which is now in the Louvre. There too, however, the old master confirms

21

the courtly aspect of his art in the highly sophisticated ivory-like illusion of the image. Duccio's version is clearly much more modern, because of his ability to combine human sentiment and agreeable form, creating a musically and pictorially vibrant image that is weightlessly suspended in the heavens.

GIOTTO.   *Madonna and Child in Majesty.*

This great panel painted at the beginning of the 14th century, which belongs stylistically between Giotto's cycles at Assisi and Padua, inaugurated a new trend in Florentine art. As revolutionary as Masaccio and Caravaggio in their times, Giotto powerfully and violently expresses here the sense of a changed conception of the world. An affirmation of an unknown truth, beyond the astonishing novelty of the pictorial invention, it inevitably involved a new ideological content and sweeping new attitudes of mind.

In this painting, perhaps the work most completely executed by the master's own hand, Giotto propounds his new realism. Man and history are no longer outside but "within" the icon, whose specialized terms are dissolved

GIOTTO DI BONDONE
Florence 1267? — Florence 1337
Madonna and Child in Majesty
(circa 1300), called the
Madonna d'Ognissanti, from the church of
Ognissanti, Florence.
Tempera on panel; 10'8" × 6'8 1/4".

GIOTTINO
Florence, active from 1324 to 1369
Pietà from S. Remigio
Tempera on panel; 6'4 3/4" × 4'4 3/4".
From the church
of the same name in Florence.
Detail: St. Benedict and S. Remigio
presenting two donors.
6th decade of the 14th century.

in the name of a living and pulsating humanity. This is a humanity that has taken its place on the throne, a concrete symbol of the terrestrial city in development, free of myths and firmly believing in itself and its own forces.

GIOTTINO. *Pietà from San Remigio.* p. 23

p. 23

To speak of Giottino, son of Stefano who was the son of a daughter of Giotto, is to speak also of the closely parallel and stylistically somewhat similar vicissitudes of at least three other great masters working in Florence in the middle of the 14th century. These are Maso (with whom Giottino has often been confused), Nardo and especially Giovanni da Milano. The third, Milano, was a purist who at the same time was open to the fascinations of the broad naturalistic interest proper to the north Italian cultural ambience from which he came. Parts of the *Polyptych from Ognissanti,* in the same room, are by Milano; and by Nardo there is a magnificent *Crucifixion.* Unfortunately nothing can be attributed to Maso with certainty. He may perhaps have been one of the artists who worked on the colossal polyptych ascribed to Bernardo Daddi, which is in the same room. Among the half-busts of saints that formerly crowned this composition, at least the two that close the rows of seven on either side have Maso's character. The works that may be catalogued as by Giottino are also very rare. The *Pietà from San Remigio* presents an open space in which the figures are balanced on a vast horizon. It descends in this respect from the urban inventions of Maso, and it has high-keyed colors derived from "Stefano Fiorentino."

SIMONE MARTINI. *Annunciation.*

One of the greatest masters, Martini has the ingratiating refinement that Petrarch admired and at the same time an impressive realism filtered through an aristocratic gentility equal only to that of Boccaccio. The artist's vitality is restrained by a sweet and skittish manner, an urban air, to use the expression applied to him by Vasari. This champion of the Sienese international style, that is of the cosmopolitan culture then being formed in Europe, with which Siena kept constantly up to date, owes a great deal to Duccio. The perennial reappearance of stylization is apparently a vocation in Sienese art over the centuries, as Martini's *Majesty* of around 1315 for the Palazzo Pubblico attests.

All of his work is developed between two poles of pictorial language. One is that of the ceremonious "Gothic," refreshed through the experience of the miniature painters, cabinet-makers and silversmiths of Paris (but also through local ones, like the Master of Fròsini) and the painters of Westminster. The other is the humanistic and narrative pole, undoubtedly repeating and following the measure of Giotto's cycle at Assisi. On the one hand, there is the *Icon of St. Louis,* and on the other the *St. Martin* frescoes at Assisi. But the figures outside the cycle in the Basilica of St. Francis already show a different ardor, an attenuated and vibrant rhythm, a challenging gesticulation enclosed in elegant form, suggesting an ancestor in Giovanni's façade in the Cathedral of Siena.

These complex features of Simone Martini's sensibility again appear prominently in this *Annunciation,* as in the miniature of Petrarch's Ambrosian

24

SIMONE MARTINI
Siena 1284 — Avignon 1344
Annunciation
Detail. Tempera on panel; 8'8 1/4" × 10'.
Executed in 1333 for the chapel of S. Ansano in the Cathedral of Siena, in collaboration with his brother-in-law, Lippo Memmi (who was responsible for the two saints at the side, which are not reproduced). The painting of *God the Father* which occupied the tondo in the upper center has been lost.

PIETRO LORENZETTI
Siena circa 1280 — Siena 1348
*The Blessed Umiltà Reading
to her Companions in the Refectory*
(dated 1316 on the central panel)
Detail of the frontal with
Scenes from the Life of the Blessed Umiltà
(the two missing scenes are in Berlin).
Tempera on panel; 17 1/2″ × 12 1/2″.

AMBROGIO LORENZETTI
Siena circa 1280 — Siena 1348
Presentation in the Temple
Tempera on panel; 8′3 1/4″ × 4′8″.
Signed and dated (in Latin): AMBROSIUS
LAURENTII FECIT HOC OPUS ANNO DOMINI
MCCCXLII ("Ambrogio Lorenzetti did this
work in the year of Our Lord 1342.").
From Siena, probably from the cathedral.

Virgil or in the *Guidoriccio da Fogliano* in the Palazzo Pubblico in Siena. Here the breadth of the horizontal development derives from the narrative style of Cavallini and the Neapolitans, and from these sources probably also comes the invention of the miraculous aspect of the figure. It appears gigantic against the lunar azure of the sky, in a desert landscape among silent rocks, as unexpected as in a Late Gothic dream. In the *Annunciation* it is a gesticulatory design that makes an arabesque in the air, almost with the mobility of gesture and the dancing rhythm of Indian sculpture. Its exoticism is also clearly shown in the Mongol types of the figures and the "Japanese" elements of the action.

AMBROGIO LORENZETTI. *Presentation in the Temple.*
This is a late work, drawn in thumb-nail line, in an archaic taste translating the analogous scene frescoed in the right transept of the Lower Church of

LORENZO MONACO
Siena circa 1370–1422
Adoration of the Magi (circa 1420)
Tempera on panel; 56 3/4″ × 69 3/4″.

St. Francis at Assisi. The latter, painted around 1320, is by a double of Giotto's who is also the author of the astonishing perspective inventions generally attributed to Ambrogio.

Nevertheless it is extremely interesting to note how this panel remains the living symbol of a continuity of pictorial language that moves on from Giotto to connect with the "Renaissance" spirit of Mantegna and Liberale da Verona. The latter undoubtedly saw it in Siena; the former shows that he reflected closely on similar examples in a work of a corresponding subject in the Uffizi.

Ambrogio Lorenzetti who makes his debut under the sign of Giotto and Arnolfo, with the *Madonna* of Vico l'Abate (1319), appears here after 20 years, having grown with the experience of his brother Pietro's works. But where the latter is occasionally dramatic and agitated, Ambrogio has an idyllic temperament, an agreeableness of feeling unknown until then, except for rare images by Giovanni Pisano. For this reason perhaps, Ambrogio remains one of the best loved and most engaging artists in history.

PIETRO LORENZETTI.   *The Blessed Umiltà Reading to Her Companions in the Refectory.*   *p. 27*

Pietro Lorenzetti is one of the great figures in 14th-century painting. His experience was very much broader than is commonly believed, as he worked not only in Siena and Florence but was also in touch with the Neapolitan

STARNINA
(GHERARDO DI JACOPO)
Active from 1387 to 1409/13
Thebaid
Tempera on panel; 6'10" × 5'9".

world. His deep beginnings, furthermore, are not under the sign of the late Duccio — even though expanded — but rather under the much more modern and articulated example of Tino da Camaino. In this work he shows a close approach to the lyrical, subdued language of his brother Ambrogio, with whom he lived in a continuous exchange of ideas.

LORENZO MONACO. *Adoration of the Magi.*

Stemming from the circle of Agnolo Daddi, Lorenzo Monaco, a Camaldolite monk from the Convento degli Angeli, conserves Sienese stylization in its most rarefied form. On it he grafts the Late Gothic atmosphere of the courts of Europe. Lorenzo Monaco accomplishes this not so much by adopting the current repertory as by carrying the style's graphic potential to a degree of extravagance and hallucination.

STARNINA. *Thebaid.*

Starnina's *Thebaid* is a large panel that represents in reduced form, tamed to suit Late Gothic middle-class taste, the saga of the Camposanto at Pisa. Yet in the fresh ingenuity of its invention, the anecdotal pleasantness and lively animation of this scene, beyond any doctrinal considerations, it is the convincing illustration of a new ideal connected with nature, with the surprise and color of life.

GENTILE DA FABRIANO. *Adoration of the Magi — Nativity.*

Gentile had the benefit of various cultural experiences during his typically "international" training, which was composite indeed, although filtered through his individualistic temperament. Not far from his birthplace there was the environment of Orvieto, characterized by sculpture, painting and enamels of a highly refined stylization, derived from Siena. Other experiences came from Gentile's relations with the illustrators of health manuals and with Venetian and Bohemian painters. Of great importance, however, was his link with Altichiero, who undoubtedly was the last great master of the 14th century in Italy. He alone could have passed on to the wandering painter from Fabriano that rediscovered humanity, so palpitating and real, which made 19th-century art historians compare him to Masaccio. The path of this influence is seen again in the development of Pisanello, which in fact was conditioned by that artist's awareness of Altichiero's work, though Pisanello's points in common with Gentile are not limited to this.

Certainly Gentile does not participate as just a professional story teller in the great renewal of vision taking place in Florence during those years. Yet he remains in an ambiguous, or rather ambivalent, position, because of the persistence in his work of arcane and visionary suggestions from the medieval epic.

This painting in any case remains of capital importance for the understanding of 15th-century Florentine art. It was executed with great care and love, and enriched with a series of highly agreeable inventions, like that of the illusionistic "hot houses" opened in the concave pilasters or that of the gold ground in the central compartment of the predella, which suggests a landscape spangled with sunshine.

GENTILE DA FABRIANO
Fabriano circa 1370 — Rome 1427
Adoration of the Magi
In the predella: *Nativity, Flight into Egypt, Presentation in the Temple;* in the pinnacles: *Annunciation* and *Christ in Majesty,* between pairs of *Prophets;* on the pilasters: leaves and flowers.
Tempera on panel; 6'8" × 9'3".
Signed and dated in Latin: OPUS GENTILIS DE FABRIANO MCCCCXXIII MENSIS MAII ("The work of Gentile da Fabriano, May 1423"). From S. Trinità, Florence, where it was in the Strozzi Chapel, and had been commissioned by Palla Strozzi.
Right: *Nativity*. Detail of the predella.

FRA ANGELICO. *Coronation of the Virgin.*

Mistakenly held to be a work of collaboration or of students (Zanobi Strozzi), this painting in fact belongs to the master's maturity. He interprets the theme of the Coronation, eschewing perspective and linear elements and adopting mobile, fluid forms — saints, angels and clouds — to create a predominantly curvilinear composition. A first statement of this is seen in the scalloped low-sprung arch that defines the upper part of the panel and at the sides joins the two compact semicircles of the figures. The heads and bodies of these figures are variously oriented, but not their halos, which are delicately decorated in relief like coins and shown flat. The surfaces of the halos, therefore, are exploited to the maximum and acquire further consistency and refulgence. Christ and the Virgin are seated on a circle of clouds, and behind them explodes a nimbus of sharp-pointed rays, indicating a limitless expansion of light and space. The equivalence of the two terms recurs frequently in Angelico's work. Here, by emphasizing the instruments played by the angels, especially the very long trumpets extending obliquely upward, he seems to be suggesting that the musical element might be inserted into the relationship.

PAOLO UCCELLO. *The Battle of San Romano.*   *pp. 34–35*

The Florentines, led by Niccolò Maurucci da Tolentino, and the Sienese, led by Bernardino della Ciarda, clashed near S. Romano on June 1, 1432. The conflict was resolved by another famous captain, Micheletto Attendolo da Cotignola, who intervened in favor of the Florentines and thus decided their victory. In three great panels commissioned by the Medici for their palace in the Via Larga, Paolo Uccello commemorated the event, placing one of the leading *condottieri* at the center of each scene. The panel in the National Gallery in London depicts the beginning of the battle, with the Florentines arrayed around Niccolò da Tolentino. The panel in the Louvre shows the unexpected arrival of Micheletto. More directly based on the combat itself, the composition in the Uffizi catches the decisive moment, when Bernardino is hit and thrown from the big white horse, which rears before the compact ranks of the enemy. In the background little groups of Sienese retreat toward the hills, pursued by Florentine archers, and in an obvious parallel, their flight is interwoven with that of the hares being chased by greyhounds across the fields.

Without dwelling on the commemorative and illustrative aspects of the theme, the artist has elaborated each form: warriors encased in armor, heavy-hoofed horses, shields, lances, trumpets, crossbows, faceted headgear, crested helmets. He has studied the degree of foreshortening in terms of the specific perspective graduation, both in the figures still involved in the conflict and in the objects and figures lying on the ground. Selecting concave or convex planes and crescent-shaped profiles, he has stripped every structure of its accidental aspects to transform it into a metaphysical component of an affray, one that is shorn of its historical significance and assimilated to an exclusively mathematical and figurative reality.

FRA ANGELICO
(FRA GIOVANNI DA FIESOLE)
Vicchio 1387. At Foligno and Cortona around 1418; subsequently active in Florence where he began the decoration of the Convento di S. Marco in 1436, and in Rome from 1447 to 1449 and from 1454 to 1455. Died in Rome in 1455.
Coronation of the Virgin
(circa 1435–1440)
Tempera on panel; 44" × 45".
From the church of S. Egidio
(later S. Maria Nuova).
Entered the Uffizi in 1825.

On pages 34–35:
PAOLO UCCELLO
(PAOLO DI DONO)
Florence 1397. After an apprenticeship with Ghiberti he went to Venice (1425–1430). Subsequently he worked in Florence, with brief periods in Padua (1445) and Urbino (1467–1469). Died in Florence in 1475.
Battle of San Romano
(circa 1456–1469)
Tempera on panel; 5'11 1/2" × 10'7".
Signed in Latin at lower left: PAULI UGELLI OPUS ("The work of Paolo Uccello"). It was in "Piero's Room" in the Palazzo Medici (later Riccardi), then in the Grand Ducal Wardrobe until 1784, when it came to the Uffizi. Companion panels with similar subjects are today in the Louvre, Paris, and the National Gallery, London.

MASACCIO AND MASOLINO. *Madonna and Child with St. Anne.*
The surface of the painting is divided into almost equal portions painted by
Masaccio (the step, the throne, the Madonna and Child, the angel holding
the curtain at upper right, perhaps the angel at the summit) and by Masolino (St. Anne, the other three angels). Yet there is no question that the
more incisive contribution is that of Masaccio. Reserving the base and the
central nucleus of the picture for himself, Masaccio was able to establish
his conception of space by means of substantial volumes articulated in
depth. These include the step with its compressed curve and the Madonna's
body expanding into space in the powerful knees, with the head firmly
joined to shoulders and back by the enwrapping motion of the veil. Another large volume is formed by the Child, which has a point of maximum
concentration where the hands of the mother have a pincers-like grip on
His thigh. Masolino evidently assented to the general scheme by supporting
the structure of the central block with the figure of St. Anne. In it he re-
spects the perspective construction with its very low viewpoint, as is shown
in the saint's suspended hand, whose palm can be seen. Only in the angels,

MASACCIO
(TOMMASO GUIDI)
Castel S. Giovanni 1401. Active in Florence
in the third decade of the century (frescoes
in the Brancacci Chapel, polyptych for the
church of the Carmine in Pisa). In 1428 he
went to Rome, where he died unexpectedly.
Madonna and Child with St. Anne
(circa 1424)
Tempera on panel; 69″ × 40 1/2″.
The work has suffered considerable damage
and in some areas is greatly altered. On the
step are inscribed the Latin words for "Hail
Mary full of Grace. The Lord be with you.
Blessed be . . ." Executed in collaboration
with Masolino for the church of S. Ambrogio, where Vasari saw it. Subsequently it
went to the Accademia, and then to the
Uffizi in 1919.

MASACCIO and MASOLINO
Madonna and Child with St. Anne
Detail of the central group

which certainly belong to him, does Masolino digress from the structural composition of the center of the painting. An example is the fragile censer that the angel at lower left swings toward the edge of the panel, as if to avoid clashing against the Virgin's mantle.

DOMENICO VENEZIANO. *Madonna and Child with SS. Francis, John the Baptist, Zenobius and Lucy.*

To understand the values achieved in this altarpiece, it is necessary to re-

DOMENICO VENEZIANO
Venice 1400/1406. Active in Perugia in 1438, in Florence at S. Egidio in 1439 and between 1441 and 1445; subsequently he also worked in Florence for the most part, but the number of paintings that has come down to us is very limited. He died in Venice in 1461.
Madonna and Child with SS. Francis, John the Baptist, Zenobius and Lucy (circa 1445–1448)
Tempera and oil(?) on panel; 6'10 1/4" × 6'11 3/4".
The Latin inscription on the step means: "The work of Domenico Veneziano. Oh Mother of God have mercy on me. Amen." The dismembered predella is distributed among the museums of Berlin (*Martyrdom of St. Lucy*), Cambridge (*Miracle of St. Zenobius, Annunciation*) and Washington (*St. John in the Desert*). Executed for the high altar of the church of S. Lucia de' Magnoli, it entered the Uffizi in 1862.

FRA FILIPPO LIPPI
Florence circa 1406. Active mainly in Florence, except for a brief stay in Padua (1434). In 1452 he executed the frescoes in the Cathedral of Prato, between 1467 and 1469 those in the Cathedral of Spoleto. He died at Spoleto in 1469.
Madonna and Child with Two Angels (about 1455–1460)
Tempera on panel; 36 1/4" × 25".
On the back is a sketch for a half-length female figure. From the Villa of Poggio Imperiale, it came to the Uffizi in 1796.

construct the complex articulation of the architectural structure. Closing off the background is a polygonal exedra with three niches in the central faces and two kiosks at the sides. Further forward a portico with pointed arches and cross vaults, carried on slim columns and resting on a stepped basement, shelters the Madonna's seat. In the foreground a lozenge-patterned pavement gives consistency to the space occupied by the four saints. Every element is defined by subtle color contrasts — of pink, yellow and light green against white. In the morning clarity, the light raining down from above transforms, as it circulates, the predominant void into concrete space. It carves the profiles and singles out the forms, and it shines on the marble,

39

the clothes and the glass halos rimmed with gold. Now the motive for the absorbed looks and the suspended gestures of the figures becomes clear. Iconographic conventions such as showing St. Francis reading and meditating, John the Baptist pointing, St. Zenobius blessing and St. Lucy proffering her plate and the palm of martyrdom, are used to emphasize the composed serenity of the silent meeting.

40

FRA FILIPPO LIPPI
Coronation of the Virgin
(circa 1441–1447)
Tempera on panel; 6'6 3/4" × 9'5".

The frame, which is the original one, has two small tondo paintings at the sides of the upper center part showing the *Annunciation*. Executed for the high altar of the church of S. Ambrogio, where it is mentioned by the old sources. In 1913 it was sold to the Accademia by the antique dealer, Volpini. It went to the Uffizi in 1919. The work is shown here during restoration.

FILIPPO LIPPI. *Madonna and Child with Two Angels.* p. 39

This painting is one of the most refined examples of 15th-century devotional art, executed probably for one of the Medici. If it was not commissioned by Cosimo the Elder, who was an affectionate and understanding client of Filippo Lippi and more than once had him pardoned for his amorous affairs, then it was ordered by one of his relatives. This work was criticized for a certain lack of unity and measure, but in reality Lippi is an artist whose imagination is too quick to kindle and an experimenter too open and too receptive to novelty, for him to be judged according to any classic formulas. He seizes every pretext to enrich pictorial reality, and he accepts, assimilates and immediately abandons any fact of experience or culture to go in pursuit of another. Thus he arrives at solutions that perhaps are lacking in rigor, but nevertheless teem with invention and have the ability to communicate flights of the imagination with exceptional immediacy. Here the stone frame seems barely able to contain the over-abundant figurative material. The composition is compressed, however, in the group of divine figures: in the pleating of the Virgin's robes and veils, and in the interlacing of the solid limbs of the Child and the angels. The most mobile elements of the latter — hands, eyes, laughing mouths — are emphasized. Silvery reflections skim the hair, the embroidery and the gems, and touch the landscape that extends in a close succession of rivers, hedges, rocky peaks and tower-crowned cities.

FILIPPO LIPPI. *Coronation of the Virgin.*

The middle arch of the three that cut the upper part of the composition is occupied at the center by a throne that is fascinating but hybrid in structure and that extends forward to occupy a good part of the cramped space. By forcing the perspective, Lippi has stretched the sides apart to reveal the elements of various stylistic derivations that make up his composition. We see cornices, pilasters, niches, volutes and pinnacles, supporting garlands and festoons of flowers, drapery and ribbons with inscriptions. In the areas at the sides, the painted bands in the background optically reduce the extent of the spaces crowded with angels carrying lilies. In the foreground are groups of saints and worshippers, with a point of maximum expansion toward the spectator in the half-figure of the angel displaying a scroll to the kneeling figure on the right. This figure is not the author of the work but the donor, Francesco di Antonio Maringhi, Canon of S. Lorenzo and chaplain of S. Ambrogio. Fra Filippo Lippi himself is represented as the Carmelite monk shown on the opposite side, resting his chin on his hand. A marked desire to exploit all the possibilities for representation to be found in figures and things has driven the artist to load the composition. He varies to the utmost the foreshortening of the heads, the attitudes and the draperies. In each of these elements a quality deriving from Masaccio persists, but otherwise they are defined by a line given to straying, though sometimes unexpectedly tense and concise, typical of Lippi. The series of more or less conventional faces is punctuated with strongly characterized portraits, such as those of the two monks, of Maringhi and of St. Teofista in front of him. At the same time the realistic detail is given nuance by the fantastic greenish light that enfolds the bizarre assembly.

PIERO DELLA FRANCESCA
Borgo San Sepolcro 1410/1420
In 1439 he was an assistant to
Domenico Veneziano in Flor-
ence; around 1450 worked in
Urbino, Ferrara, Rimini; between
1452 and 1459 painted the fres-
coes in San Francesco, Arezzo.
After a visit to Rome in 1459 he
worked principally in Urbino and
Borgo San Sepolcro, where he
died in 1492.

Triumphal Diptych (*Federico Il da Montefeltro* and *Battista Sforza*) (circa 1465)
Tempera and oil on panel; 18″ × 13″.
The surface of the painting has yellowed because of deterioration in the glazes. Formerly in the ducal palace of Urbino, it came to Florence with the Della Rovere inheritance and entered the Uffizi in 1773.

CLARVS INSIGNI VEHITVR TRIVMPHO ·
QVEM PAREM SVMMIS DVCIBVS PERHENNIS ·
FAMA VIRTVTVM CELEBRAT DECENTER ·
SCEPTRA TENENTEM ↝

PIERO DELLA FRANCESCA. *Triumphal Diptych.*   *pp. 42–45*

The famous diptych of the rulers of Urbino includes the representation of Duke Federico II (1422–1482) and his wife Battista Sforza (1446–1472) on the two faces. On the back the same subjects are shown riding in triumphal cars, with Federico accompanied by the cardinal virtues and crowned by Victory; while Battista, escorted by the theological virtues and other allegorical figures, is drawn by a pair of unicorns, symbolizing chastity. In showing the two figures on the obverse of the panel in profile — aside from the practical reason that the duke had lost an eye — the artist wished to underscore the commemorative nature of the picture by associ-

QVE MODVM REBVS TENVIT SECVNDIS ·
CONIVGIS MAGNI DECORATA RERVM ·
LAVDE GESTARVM VOLITAT PER ORA ·
CVNCTA VIRORVM

PIERO DELLA FRANCESCA
Triumphal Diptych, detail of the
two Triumphs painted on the back.
The Latin inscription below *Federico's Triumph,* interpreted freely, says that an illustrious vehicle for a signal triumph re-
lates him to the supreme and eternal military
leaders; the fame of his virtue does honor
to him, who holds the scepter.
According to the inscription below *Battista's
Triumph,* only the fact that she was a
woman put her in second place, as an adorn-
ment to her great husband; praise of her
deeds wings from mouth to mouth; she belongs to the breed of illustrious men.

ating it with the tradition of medal design. This is confirmed by the Saphic
strophes in Latin painted at the base of the two triumphs in large capital
letters. Piero, however, does not accept indiscriminately the stylistic modes
connected with the representation of figures in profile, which were graphic
and linear even in the illustrious examples of Pisanello. He gives volumetric
definition to the faces and shoulders, concentrating the value of the forms
in a few key elements, such as Federico's cylindrical hat, and the collar and
medallions on Battista's head and breast. The structures emerge in absolute immobility, scanned along their sharp contours and curved planes by a
uniformly diffused, hard, clear light. As a consequence there is a certain de-

tachment from the landscape, which is partially hidden and extends into an indefinite distance. On the reverse, the countryside is identical but plays a more important part, as the cars do not stand out against it but travel along it, permitting the viewer to follow more readily the extent of the misty valleys, the succession of hills, the course of the roads and the reflecting sheets of water.

The work belongs to the artist's maturity, when he was about to devote himself predominantly to speculative thought (he was to dedicate his treatise on perspective in painting to Federico). It is perhaps the most famous work of that splendid civilization of Urbino that brought together personalities like Piero, Leon Battista Alberti, Luca Pacioli and Francesco di Giorgio.

ALESSIO BALDOVINETTI. *Annunciation.*

Baldovinetti, a first class painter and artisan, was an expert in luxurious stuffs and goldsmith's work (his pictures tell us), as well as a mosaicist and a supplier of cartoons for inlaid wood and stained glass. He expresses himself in highly controlled terms in this youthful *Annunciation,* which reveals his study of Domenico Veneziano and that artist's "colored perspective." As the white slabs of the pavement in the portico show, the focal point is not situated on the central axis of the panel, but to the left, above the angel. The dominant verticality is confirmed by the proportions of the figures and the lectern, and by the prominence given to the columns and the cypresses. The filigree of the two protagonists' blond hair and the reds and blue violets of the velvet are expressions of Baldovinetti's refined taste. Another instance is the unusual pavement, which is made up not of tiles laid in a geometrical pattern, but of an irregular succession of white, green, pink and azure blotches and veinings.

GIOVANNI BELLINI. *Pietà*   p. 48

The work was attributed to Bellini by Cavalcaselle (1871) and most critics agree in considering it a notable painting by the master.

A reason for the disagreement is the unusual technique, because of which Gronau (1935) is inclined to believe that it is not a finished work but one in preparation and was still to be colored. Others, like Van Marle (1935) consider it to be a completed work. This is the more credible opinion, given its formal development, almost as if Bellini had wanted to show his ability to suggest a fullness of image and feeling in monochrome. In any case, the use of monochrome has a long tradition. Here, however, we are not dealing with the simulated bas-reliefs that were so dear to Mantegna, for instance. Bellini resolves every problem of the plasticity of bodies and the atmosphere of the setting with a subtlety of chiaroscuro as rigorous as in Dürer.

The complexity of the composition, with many figures solemnly and harmoniously disposed around the lifeless body of Christ, presupposes a notable experience. As we know that from 1480 Bellini was working on a large canvas in the Ducal Palace in Venice, it seems reasonable to place this *Pietà* after those in Stuttgart and Toledo, thus dating it around 1495.

ALESSIO BALDOVINETTI
Florence 1427. Pupil of Fra Angelico, he always worked in Florence. Active around 1466 in the Chapel of the Cardinal of Portugal in S. Miniato al Monte. Died in Florence in 1499.
Annunciation (circa 1445–1450)
Tempera on panel; 65 3/4" × 54".
Executed for the church of S. Giorgio alla Costa, it subsequently was moved to the Convento di S. Spirito. It entered the Uffizi Gallery in 1868.

GIOVANNI BELLINI. *Sacred Allegory.*

Certainly this is one of the most fascinating paintings of the 15th century in Italy, not only because of its beauty of form but also because of the mystery of its meaning. Cavalcaselle, who attributed it to Bellini (1871), understood the difficulty of interpreting the picture. In fact, despite Ludwig's attempt (1907) to identify the subject with that of the "Souls in Purgatory" in *Pélérinage de l'âme,* the little medieval poem by Guillaume Deguileville — which was correctly confuted by Rasmo (1946) — we are still not in a position to explain this grouping of saints around the Holy Family, on a neat marble terrace. St. Paul stands outside the white balustrade. St. Job and St. Sebastian are in the act of adoring the Child, who is playing with some other children. A young woman wearing a crown prays beside the throne of the Madonna, while a woman wrapped in a mantle appears to be watching over the children's game. Undoubtedly in the future other suggestions about the meaning of the subject will be added to those of Verdier (*Allegory of Justice and Mercy,* 1952) and Braunfeld (*Representation of Paradise,* 1956), as religious and mythological allusions are undeniably present. For instance, note the centaur, who makes a pendant to the shepherd resting on the bank of the mysterious river overlooked by the terrace with its Lombard-style inlaid marble pavement. In the formal distribution of the figures in the space, there is an evident break. In the foreground, in an atmosphere of suspension, the clear morning light quietly caresses liv-

GIOVANNI BELLINI
Venice circa 1430 — Venice 1516
Pietà (circa 1495)
Panel (monochrome); 30″ × 47 1/2″.
It is not known for whom the work was painted. Alvise Mocenigo bought it from the Aldobrandini Gallery in Rome, and presented it to the Grand Duke of Tuscany in 1798.

GIOVANNI BELLINI
Sacred Allegory (circa 1490)
Panel; 28 3/4″ × 47″.
This little panel entered the Uffizi in 1795,
having come from the Villa of Poggio Imperiale. It had been there since 1783, when
the Abbot Lanzi, who was in charge of the
Grand Duke's collections, acquired it in an
exchange with the Imperial Collections in
Vienna. The little trees standing out on the
heights are 16th-century additions (Longhi).

ing beings and things: the mysterious woman mantled in her everyday gar-
ment, as well as the fallen fruit that the little child bends to pick up. In the
landscape background, in the recurrent alternation of time, men are awak-
ening and starting their daily tasks.

ANDREA MANTEGNA. *The Madonna of the Quarry.* p. 50

As there are no external factors for dating this unusual work, a resort to
formal analysis is opportune, and this substantially corroborates Vasari, who
put it at the end of the 1480s. After the superb series of the *Triumphs* for
Mantua, which had immersed him in an evocation of antiquity, Mantegna
in this meditative work appears to follow an almost Bellinian vein of intimacy, calming his earlier taste for dissonant colors. Vasari's description
shows the writer's admiration for that age in which artists "were subtly in-
vestigating, and after much study imitating, the true property of natural
things." That Mantegna was attracted to geological phenomena is shown
as early as in the backgrounds of his work in the Capella Ovetari, in Padua,
where he multiplies some modest aspect of the Euganean quarries, as if in
"symbolic accord." Perhaps the contract between the geometrically splin-
tered peak and the sweet pensive Madonna holding her Child is enough to

ANDREA MANTEGNA
Isola di Carturo (Padua) 1431
— Mantua 1506
Adoration of the Magi (circa 1460)
Concave panel; 30″ × 30″.
The earliest and most reliable documentation of this painting goes back to 1587, when it was in the Villa Muggia (Pistoia) belonging to Don Antonio de' Medici, son of Bianca Cappello. It was accompanied also at that time by the two wings showing the *Ascension* and the *Presentation in the Temple* or *Circumcision*. It is disputed whether the three panels were originally intended to go together. but subsequently the triptych was dismembered and was only put together again in 1887. Longhi believes that the original right-hand wing was the *Death of the Virgin* in the Prado. It is likely that the composition, along with other paintings, adorned the chapel of the Castello di San Giorgio, which Mantegna started to decorate around 1459.

ANDREA MANTEGNA
The Madonna of the Quarry
Panel; 12 1/2″ × 11 3/4″.
Vasari cites the painting as being "in the home of the most illustrious Signor Don Francesco de' Medici, Prince of Florence" and states that it was executed in Rome (thus between 1488 and 1490). As it is not in the inventory of Lorenzo de' Medici's possessions, compiled in 1494, it is unlikely that the work was done for him. While some scholars accept Vasari's statement, Knapp suggests a date between 1466 and 1467 when Mantegna stayed in Florence and Pisa and could have seen quarrymen at work around Carrara. Kristeller, however, maintains that the rock behind the Madonna is not marble but the basalt found in the Veneto.

explain the secret of the work. However, F. Hartt (1952) has pushed the contrast to signify a complex allegory of the old Law, now sterile, and the new Law, given life by Christ and the Virgin.

ANDREA MANTEGNA. *Adoration of the Magi.*

In the absence of any sure documentation, it is the internal evidence of the forms that suggest the date of the work. The accurately dated painting closest to it is the great *Polyptych of San Zeno,* completed in 1459. Of course the comparison is best made with the scenes in the predella, especially for the relationship between figures and environment. In this *Adoration,* Mantegna is seeking a humanistic balance for the fabulous and picturesque aspects of the Gothic cavalcades. His taste for geology prompts him to center attention on the Madonna and the kings paying homage, with the dark background of the cave going back into a fanciful rock, alive with cherubim. While the definition of forms is always vigorous and typological, the artist does not slacken the tension in evoking a clear, luminous atmosphere.

ANDREA MANTEGNA. *The Circumcision.* p. 52

In the present arrangement of the triptych, the position of this right wing is questioned by scholars, who point out that the disposition of the interior of this elaborate Renaissance chapel (Tietze sees an affinity with the Cappella del Perdono in Urbino, by Laurana) does not fit well with the other two scenes in the open. A unitary program was recognized by Saxl (1938–1939), who maintains that the subject is a *Presentation in the Temple,* because of the Biblical scenes represented in the lunettes. The figures are drawn and colored with a subtle fineness that must have delighted Mantegna's brother-in-law, Giovanni Bellini. His angel in the almost contemporary *Blood of the Redeemer,* in London, has its origin here.

52

ANDREA MANTEGNA
The Circumcision or
Presentation in the Temple
(circa 1462–1464)
Panel; 33 3/4″ × 16 3/4″.
With the *Assumption,* the little panel makes
up — in a 19th-century frame — a triptych
already composed in this way in 1587, when
it was in a villa near Pistoia belonging to
Don Antonio de' Medici. Perhaps with other
pieces it was part of the decoration of the
chapel of the Castello di San Giorgio, which
Mantegna began around 1459. Perhaps this
panel belongs to the "little works" Mantegna
mentions in a letter in 1464 as "to be var-
nished," indicating that they had just been
finished.

ANDREA MANTEGNA
Portrait of Cardinal Carlo de' Medici
(circa 1466)
Panel; 16" × 11 1/2".
The painting is in such a bad state of preservation that Kristeller decidedly, and Tietze with some reservation, questioned its authenticity. However, the positive opinions of Berenson, Suida and Fiocco have oriented the majority of critics toward including the portrait in the corpus of Mantegna's works. The subject was identified by Emil Shaffer (1912) from the engraving of the Medici family tree by Martino Rota.

ANDREA MANTEGNA. *Cardinal Carlo de' Medici.*
The identification of the subject as Cardinal Carlo de' Medici is important in confirming a date for the work suggested by stylistic analysis. It is likely that the painting was executed in 1466, when Mantegna is known to have gone to Florence. The vigorous image of the subject, in which our attention is centered on the sculpturally prominent physical features, foreshadows the extraordinary series of dignified portrayals of the Gonzagas that Mantegna was to do in Mantua.

ANTONIO AND PIERO POLLAIOLO. *SS. Eustace, James and Vincent.*
In honor of Cardinal James of Lusitania, nephew of the King of Portugal,
who died at the age of 25 in Florence, Bishop Alvarez decided to establish
a funeral chapel in his memory at S. Miniato al Monte. It was designed by
Antonio Manetti and decorated by Luca della Robbia, Antonio Rosselino,
Baldovinetti and the Pollaiolo brothers. The altarpiece, now substituted in
the church by a copy, represents the cardinal's patron saints, and is one of
the first examples of the collaboration between Antonio and Piero Pollaiolo.
As is always the case, the contribution of the former is dominant, while the

ANTONIO POLLAIOLO
(ANTONIO BENCI)
Florence circa 1431. Active in Florence as
goldsmith, painter and sculptor until 1489,
when he went to Rome, where he died.
SS. Eustace, James and Vincent
(1467–1468). Tempera and
oil (?) on panel; 67 3/4″ × 70 1/2″.
Executed in collaboration with Pollaiolo's
brother, Piero, for the altar of the chapel
built by Bishop Alfonso Alvarez for the
tomb of James of Lusitania, Archbishop of
Lisbon and Cardinal of S. Eusachio, who
died in Florence in 1459. Moved to the Uffizi in 1800.

ANTONIO POLLAIOLO
*The Labors of Hercules: Hercules and
the Hydra, Hercules and Antaeus*
(circa 1470)
Oil on panel; 7″ × 4 3/4″ and 6 1/4″
× 3 3/4″ respectively. Carried off during
World War II, they were recovered in Amer-
ica recently and restored.

latter docilely follows his lead, although he is not incapable of expressing his own personal orientation. Antonio, inventor of the pictorial scheme, worked out the presentation of the three saints in an original way. They are placed on a balcony paved with marble slabs that ties in with the mosaic floor of the chapel and the inlaid steps to the altar. A bronze grating supported by the colonettes limits the extent of the balcony, but does not block the view of the sloping landscape furrowed with streams. The imposing figures of the saints are clad in ample robes embroidered in gold and gems, in accordance with the taste of the Burgundian and Spanish courts. It is probably here that the hand of Pietro prevails, as he was more concerned than Antonio with the ideals of craftsmanship that were also held by his master, Alessio Baldovinetti.

ANTONIO POLLAIOLO. *The Labors of Hercules.*

The myth of Hercules, considered as a man at the height of his physical and mental powers, rather than as a demigod, fascinated Pollaiolo. In Hercules

ANDREA DEL VERROCCHIO (ANDREA DI CIONE) (workshop of)
Florence 1436. He directed a very active workshop, which produced painting, sculpture, goldsmith work, etc. Active in Florence until 1479, when he left for Venice to execute the Monument to Bartolomeo Colleoni. He died at Venice in 1488.
Baptism of Christ (circa 1470–1475)
Tempera and oil on panel;
69 1/2″ × 59 1/2″.
Executed for the church of S. Salvi, it was subsequently moved to the Monastery of S. Verdiana. In 1810 it went to the Accademia, and in 1914 to the Uffizi.

he saw an expression of the pure force of nature, conceived as a total and self-sufficient reality. He was a being who took part in the multifarious life of man, but was also ready to fight its bestial aspects. Antonio depicted the hero's adventures in three large panels, painted for Lorenzo de' Medici, in the small bronze in the Bargello, in the *Rape of Dejanira* at Yale and the two little panels in the Uffizi. The last repeat on a very small scale and with some variations, two of the three large *Labors* painted for Lorenzo the Magnificent in 1460, which were lost but are known in part through Robetta's prints. Probably in these later versions the dynamic aspect of the struggle is less striking, with the artist aiming more for light and color values. Note the subtlety of the tonal gradation between the yellowish stones, the brown and clotted underbrush of the broad landscape, and the dry, brown, shaggy nudes. The glint of a leaf, the reflection of a strip of water, reappear in the gleaming flash of the teeth and the burning eyes of the combatants.

WORKSHOP OF ANDREA DEL VERROCCHIO. *Baptism of Christ*.

The work has been the subject of thorough investigations, which have ascertained its composite stylistic characteristics. Very likely the panel entered Verrocchio's workshop with the stiff dove and the clumsy hands of God the Father already painted in. Completion would have been entrusted to the young artists who crowded Andrea's studio. His own activity as a painter is problematical, and it seems likely that his collaborators will be recognized as having had a predominant hand in the works attributed to him. The Baptism was then laid out according to a traditional scheme calling for symmetrical rocky outcrops at the sides, Christ in the middle, the Baptist and the group of angels as supporting wings. At this phase it seems possible to single out the participation of Botticelli, especially in the Baptist, in the angel turning to the left and in the drawing of Christ. This structure, which is still partially visible under the superimposed layers of color and varnish, was upset by another student, Leonardo da Vinci. He cut down the panel on the left, eliminating the central axis of the dove and Christ, making the composition asymmetrical, erasing one of the two rocky spurs and opening out a landscape of steep valleys, peaks and splashing water. The same transparent washes of color that make the reflections fluid and mobile attenuate the forms of Christ and run along the head and robes of the angel in profile, which traditionally is attributed to Leonardo.

On page 58:
SANDRO BOTTICELLI
(ALESSANDRO FILIPEPI)
Florence 1445. Student of Filippo Lippi, he worked mainly in Florence. From 1481 to 1482 he was in Rome for the decoration of the Sistine Chapel. He died in Florence in 1510.
Judith's Return to Bethulia
(circa 1470–1475)
Tempera on panel; 12 1/4″ × 9 1/2″.
With the *Discovery of the Body of Holofernes* (Uffizi) it made up the diptych that Rodolfo Sirigatti in 1580 gave Bianca Cappello, the wife of Francesco I, Grand Duke of Tuscany. It came to the Uffizi with the legacy of Bianca's son, Don Antonio de' Medici (1632).

SANDRO BOTTICELLI. *Judith's Return to Bethulia.* p. 58

With its twin panel this work made up a diptych typifying a variety of devotional painting for private use. It shows a mixture of references to Lippi, as well as to the circle of Verrocchio, and deeper influences from Pollaiolo. Each element, however, is turned to use within a rhythm constructed autonomously, with diagonal lines of direction stretching from foreground to background. The slaying of Holofernes has already taken place, but has left no trace on the dress or the face of Judith, who advances with her maid almost dancing along the height that dominates a valley full of soldiers. The undulations of the figures and the veils, the curves of the sword, the branch and the basket extend in the opposite direction from the path of the two girls, as if to make their motion more incisive.

SANDRO BOTTICELLI. *Self-Portrait (?) with Medal.*
The youth was first identified with various members of the Medici family —
the medal represents the Father of his Country, Cosimo the Elder — then
with Antonio Filipepi, Botticelli's brother and a medal maker, and finally
with Sandro Botticelli himself, who certainly had good reasons for professing
his fidelity to the Medici. The last identification seems the most credible
when the picture is compared to other presumed portraits of the artist.
Further support for this view comes from the pose of the head and the direction of the glance, which suggest a painter looking in a mirror. It is an intense, almost aggressive work, in the definition of the face and in the boney
quality of the hands closed around the gilt medal.

SANDRO BOTTICELLI. *St. Augustine in his Study.*
This is another work intended for private devotion. The cell, decorated with
classicizing stuccos in the late 15th-century taste, is constructed on a regular
perspective system. Diagonals converge on the central axis; the spectator's

SANDRO BOTTICELLI
Self-Portrait (?) with Medal (circa 1470)
Tempera on panel; 22 3/4″ × 17 1/4″.
It entered the Uffizi with the legacy of Car-
dinal Carlo de' Medici.

SANDRO BOTTICELLI
St. Augustine in His Study
(circa 1490–1500)
Tempera on panel; 16 1/4″ 10 1/2″.
It was seen by Vasari and Borghini in the
home of the Vecchietti family. Subsequently it belonged to the Hugford and Pieralli
collections. It came to the Uffizi in 1779.

SANDRO BOTTICELLI
La Primavera (*Spring*) (Circa 1475–1478)
Tempera on panel; 10′3 1/2″ × 7′8″.
Like the *Birth of Venus* it was executed for
a room in the Villa di Castello, recently acquired by Lorenzo di Pierfrancesco, a cousin
of Lorenzo the Magnificent belonging to a
cadet branch of the Medici family, whose
teachers were the philosopher Marsilio Ficino and other members of the Accademia
di Careggi. Botticelli illustrated Dante's *Divine Comedy* for the same patron. On Lorenzo's death the painting, and the villa,
went to Giovanni delle Bande Nere. In 1815
it was moved to the Uffizi, then to the Accademia and back again to the Uffizi in 1919.

eye should be at this height, as the view from below the tabletop indicates. Impatient, however, of a system anchoring every form to symmetry, the artist introduces an oblique thrust into the space, which determines the position of the saint's knees and head. It is reinforced by the angle of the book and the curtain drawn aside toward the exterior.

SANDRO BOTTICELLI. *La Primavera* (Spring)   *pp. 60–63*

The most persuasive interpretation of the allegorical meaning of the work, despite numerous alternative proposals, remains that in which the passage from one figure to another is seen as the progressive sublimation of sensual love in intellectual contemplation. This is a process in accordance with the harmony which governs the cosmos, and which is here evoked in the figure of Venus. The cycle, of Neo-platonic inspiration, is based on symbols and episodes in classical literature, from Hesiod to Ovid, as well as on contemporary interpretations such as those of Leon Battista Alberti and Marsilio Ficino. It begins on the right, where Zephyrus (the West Wind) pursues and seizes Chloris, the nymph who will be transformed into Flora, mother of flowers. At the center, through the mediation of Eros and Venus — Ficino's

Venus Humanitas who arouses passion but also converts it into contemplative activity — the passage to the Three Graces is effected. This triad is an ancient symbol of liberality (Aglaia who gives, Euphrosyne who receives, Thalia who returns), and in the most properly Platonic sense alludes to the relationship between the divine element and the human. On the left, Mercury dispersing clouds marks the definitive arrival of the spiritual moment. Put in these terms the program of the picture, probably elaborated at the Accademia di Careggi for Lorenzo di Pierfrancesco, appears pedantic. But Botticelli cut off the didactic embellishments, leaving the solution to the picture's extrinsic meaning enigmatic, and still controversial.

SANDRO BOTTICELLI.   *Adoration of the Magi.*

A work already celebrated and minutely described — with some contradictions — in the earliest sources, its figures are identified as Cosimo the Elder (kneeling before the Child), Piero the Gouty (in a red cloak) and Lorenzo the Magnificent, with Politian and Pico della Mirandola on the far left, and Botticelli himself at the far right. Besides these, there are Giuliano de' Medici (standing in the first row on the right) and behind him the donor, Giovanni di Zanobi del Lama, who looks toward the spectator. The Medici court is shown outside of historical reality, transposed into a living picture that is splendid in its jewel-like colors and broad scale.

SANDRO BOTTICELLI.   *Adoration of the Magi.*

A theme the artist illustrated in many variations, this is probably his last *Adoration*. Although it contains numerous references to the compositions that preceded it, there is also an evident commitment to certain new aspects of Leonardo's art, with Filippino Lippi as intermediary. This is seen in the spreading of the semicircles of figures around the masses of stratified rocks, splitting up the view of the background into broad channels and dramatizing the relationships. Perhaps this attempt failed to satisfy Botticelli, who at this time slowed down his activity, for the work remains unfinished.

SANDRO BOTTICELLI.   *Madonna of the Pomegranate.*   p. 66

The border of lilies decorating the frame, which is original, shows that the work was executed for a public building. Accordingly it has been proposed that the picture be identified with the one that Botticelli painted for an audience hall in the Palazzo Vecchio. It is a cerebral exercise on the theme of the Madonna and Child in relation to a round format. Circular devices are repeated in the golden disk raining thin golden rays, and in the semicircle of angels linked by a garland of roses and enlaced by the long sensitive hands. It is even echoed in the round form of the pomegranate, which is the symbolic and actual fulcrum of the work, and has provided its title. Along with these evident components, there are oblique thrusts and sliding movements that cannot be related to any geometrical formulas, such as the irregular oval rhythms of the scarf around the Madonna's shoulders, which is then amplified in the form of her long arms.

SANDRO BOTTICELLI. *Madonna of the Magnificat.*

The title of the tondo comes from the psalm which the Virgin is tracing out with a pen on the book supported by angels. The group is seated by a round window, whose heavy *pietra serena* frame closes and stabilizes a complex compositional structure. In the lower part of the picture it is developed in a succession of volutes and arabesques, in separate and fragmentary episodes, as in the juxtaposition of the Virgin's and Child's hands on the pomegranate,

66

SANDRO BOTTICELLI
Madonna of the Pomegranate (circa 1487)
Tempera on panel (tondo);
56 1/2″ in diameter.
Executed for the audience hall of the Magistrato dei Massai in Palazzo della Signoria. Subsequently in Cardinal Leopoldo de' Medici's collection, it moved to the Grand Ducal Wardrobe and then to the Uffizi (1780).

SANDRO BOTTICELLI
Madonna of the Magnificat
(circa 1483–1485)
Tempera on panel (tondo);
46 1/2″ in diameter.
It was sold to the Gallery in 1785 by Ottavio Magherini. In a poor state of preservation because of the removal of surface glazes.

or in the suspended complicity of the Virgin's other hand and that of the angel proffering an inkwell. The upper part is cut ruthlessly by the profiled angels placed at the edges, and opens up asymmetrically to reveal a bit of green countryside and pale sky. Farther above, there is the fleeting luminous reflections in a delicate crown of stars, in the gold-embroidered veil and in the flat rayed star bearing the symbol of the Holy Ghost.

SANDRO BOTTICELLI
Birth of Venus
(circa 1480–1485)
Tempera on canvas;
5'7 3/4" × 9'1 1/2".
Painted for a room in the Villa
di Castello (see *La Primavera*),
it went to the Uffizi in 1815.

SANDRO BOTTICELLI. *Birth of Venus.* pp. *68–70*

Various interpretations have also been proposed for this work. All, however, are connected with the birth or apparition of Venus and the classical theme of the Anadyomene, or the goddess who rises from the sea foam. The canvas was placed in a room of the Villa di Castello, the residence of Lorenzo di Pierfrancesco, where it hung with the *Primavera* and perhaps also with *Pallas and the Centaur*. The landscape, reduced to a limpid abstraction in the rippled stretch of sea, the grassy banks and the tree trunks dappled with gold, sustains the motion of the figures. It flows from the impetus of the winds arriving on outspread wings in a vortex of flowers, to the goddess, who has drifted past the central axis of the picture. Her hip goes forward in a long curve that is echoed by the thick mass of her hair. The thrust of the compositional motion is slowed down in the drapery with its resonant pleats, and in the robe and undone braids of the nymph, who is raised above the ground by the puff of wind.

SANDRO BOTTICELLI. *The St. Barnabas Altarpiece.*

Commissioned by the guild of doctors and druggists for the high altar of the church of St. Barnabas, this altarpiece differs from contemporary examples in its large size and in the complexity of its architectural background. Included in this background are elaborate marble revetments, rich stucco work and a sumptuous canopy. John the Baptist (in red, third from right) is an idealized self-portrait.

SANDRO BOTTICELLI
St. Barnabas Altarpiece: Madonna and Child with Four Angels and SS. Catherine, Augustine, Barnabas, John the Baptist, Ignatius and Michael
(circa 1490)
Tempera on panel; 8′9 1/2″ × 9′2 1/4″.
On the step of the throne are the words in Italian meaning "VIRGIN MOTHER DAUGHTER OF YOUR SON" from canto XXXIII of Dante's *Paradise*. Executed for the high altar of the church of S. Barnaba, where it remained until the suppression of religious orders under Napoleon (1808), after which it was moved to the Accademia and then to the Uffizi (1919). In 1717 a strip was added at the top to complete the panel almost to the center of the arch, probably to make up for a previous reduction of the picture. This addition has now been removed. Of the seven panels originally composing the predella, four remain at the Uffizi Gallery: *Scenes from the Lives of Christ, St. Augustine, St. Ignatius, St. John the Baptist.*

SANDRO BOTTICELLI. *Calumny.*

Densely charged with historical and cultural references and allegorical content, this work is no less complex in form. It is rich in dramatic contrasts heightened by the deep bronze and red tonalities, and the composition is characterized by the structure of the classicizing portico. The theme was treated by Apelles in a famous painting described by Lucian. It depicts the scene of a youth dragged before King Midas by Calumny, accompanied by Deceit, Fraud, and Envy. Ignorance and Suspicion whisper into the king's ass's ears, which symbolize the judge's bad conscience. On the left are Penitence, cloaked in black, and Truth, who is chaste and nude.

SANDRO BOTTICELLI. *Annunciation.*

This is a meticulous example of the master's late work, and perhaps was finished by one of his students. The surroundings are severe, rigorously measured off by the grey walls and the pavement of red tiles edged with white. Immobile, the silvery green-blue landscape extends into the distance beyond the door. In contrast, the angel kneeling on the ground and the Virgin, swaying in deference, are enveloped in ample robes irregularly swelled by the wind, which emphasizes the barely repressed movement.

SANDRO BOTTICELLI
Calumny (circa 1495)
Tempera on panel; 24 1/2″ × 35 3/4″.
Executed for Antonio Segni (according to Vasari), it subsequently went to the Pitti Palace and then to the Uffizi (1773). In composing the picture Botticelli probably followed the text of Lucian's *De Calumnia* rather than the less detailed summary given by Alberti in his *De Pictura.*

SANDRO BOTTICELLI
Annunciation (1489–1490)
Tempera on panel; 59″ × 61 1/2″.
In the lower part of the frame, which is original, a small *Pietà* is inserted. Painted for the Guardi Chapel in the church of Cestello (S. Maria Maddelena de' Pazzi); the books of that monastery have a record of the commission. It came to the Uffizi in 1872.

PIETRO PERUGINO
(PIETRO VANNUCCI)
Città della Pieve in 1445. A very active
painter, he worked principally in Umbria,
the Marches, Florence and Rome. In 1481
and 1482 he took part, perhaps also direct-
ing the work, in the decoration of the Sis-
tine Chapel. In 1505 he collaborated on the
decoration of Isabella Gonzaga's studiolo.
He died at Fontignano in 1523.
*Madonna and Child between SS. John the
Baptist and Sebastian* (dated 1493)
Oil (?) on panel; 70″ × 64 1/2″.
Signed and dated in Latin on the base of the
throne: PETRUS PERUSINUS PINXIT. AN.
MCCCCXXXXIII ("Pietro Perugino painted it
in 1493"). Commissioned by Cornelia Sal-
viati for the family chapel in S. Domenico at
Fiesole, which was later owned by the
Guadagni family. In 1786 it came to the
Uffizi and a modern copy replaced it in the
church.

PIETRO PERUGINO. *Madonna and Child Between SS. Sebastian and John the Baptist.*

The composition is rigorously articulated. Very close in the foreground is the rectangular base supporting the Virgin's unadorned bench. A little far-ther back stand the two saints, while behind them rises the first pair of pillars, followed at a more marked distance by others, indicated above in the cross vault and below in the tiled pavement. Perugino's apprenticeship with Piero della Francesca is apparent, but he also reveals that he is familiar with the latest developments in Florence, from Pollaiolo to Verrocchio, and that he is in touch with Luca Signorelli. Although this type of composition is anticipated in other examples of his early maturity, the artist achieves a special quality in this work by isolating the components, particularly the composed figures standing in the foreground. Significant in this respect is St. Sebastian, with his polished limbs.

PIETRO PERUGINO. *Pietà.*

The composition, in plan and elevation, does not vary much with respect to the preceding altarpiece, except for an accentuation of the architectural membering, which is sharper-edged and fuller. In part the group of figures differs, not so much in the increased number of subjects as in the connect-

PIETRO PERUGINO
Pietà (circa 1493)
Oil (?) on panel; 69 1/4″ × 66 1/4″.
Christ is supported by the Madonna, St.
John the Evangelist and Mary Magdalen; at
the sides stand Nicodemus and Joseph of
Arimathea. Executed for the church of S.
Giusto of the Ingesuati, near Florence; after
the demolition of the monastery it was
moved to the church of S. Giovannino della
Calza at Porta Romana, then to the Villa of
Poggio Imperiale. Requisitioned by the
French in 1799, it was later returned and
placed in the Pitti Palace; subsequently it
was moved to the Accademia and finally to
the Uffizi in 1919.

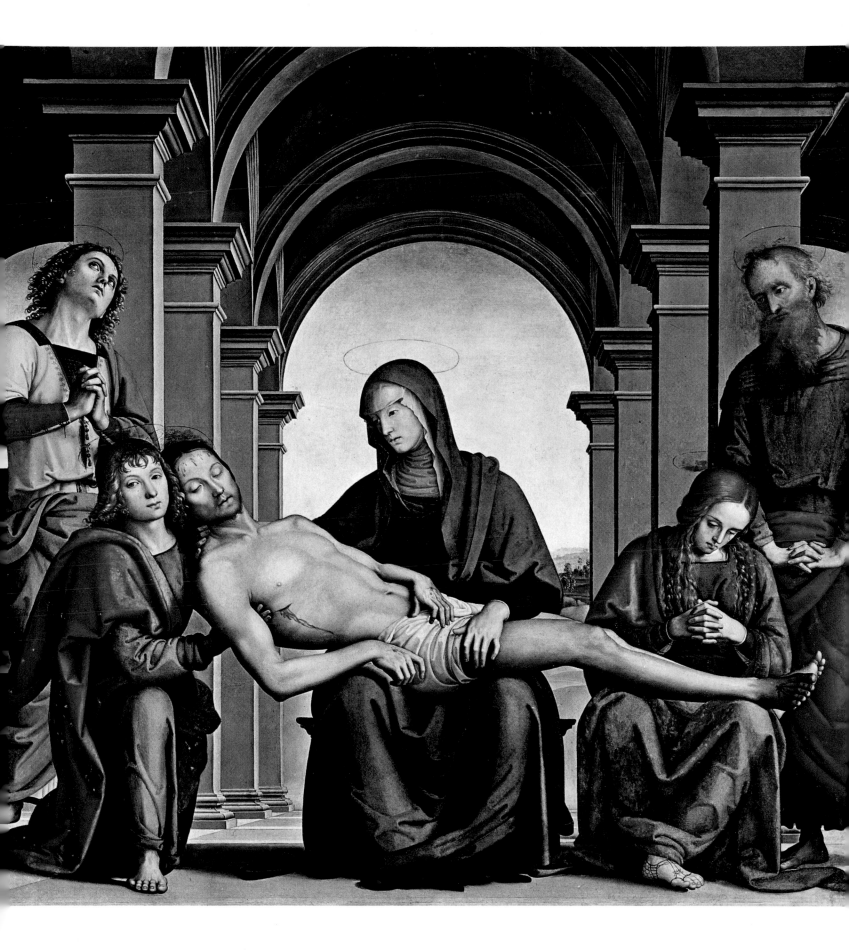

ing links that the artist felt it was necessary to introduce. Furthermore, the Pietà theme implied a degree of communication among the figures, which Perugino still managed to contain within limited terms. Placing the two standing saints to the rear, he brought forward the group of the Madonna flanked by St. John and the Magdalen. The three figures are constructed on a balanced system. St. John's shoulder is in line with his elbow and knee. The Madonna's arms and legs are arranged in an oval rhythm that includes her barely lowered head. The Magdalen is gathered into a structure that is bound together at the joined hands and ankles. On this triple pedestal the body of Christ is placed. In harmony with the cohesiveness of the composition, the body rests without bending on the Apostle's shoulder, the Mother's lap — notice the conjunction of the three hands — and the Magdalen's knees. Vasari perhaps felt that certain external aspects of the theme had been neglected, and he wrote: ". . . among other things he made a Christ in the lap of Our Lady . . . so stiffened as if the time he had been on the cross and the cold had reduced him to this."

PIETRO PERUGINO. *Portrait of a Boy.*

This portrait is of an unknown boy; its former identification with Alessandro Braccesi, secretary to the Ten of the Florentine Republic, has proved to be erroneous. It is an example of extraordinary virtuosity in the colors that defines the compact oval of the face, the pink and white skin and the dark shining eyes. The composition is subtly constructed from the oblique placing of the shoulders and the slight turn of the head, which stands out against a dark ground. The absorbed glance and the melancholy curve of the mouth reveal the painter's taste for psychological portrayal.

DOMENICO GHIRLANDAIO. *Adoration of the Magi.*

The interpretation of this subject within a round format had already been attempted by Fra Angelico, Domenico Veneziano and Botticelli. Domenico Ghirlandaio ventured on this effort only once and rather late in his career, as if it were a personal challenge. He adapted the system of the famous Botticelli tondo in the National Gallery, London — the point of departure of numerous variations — to his own specific needs. He brought the planes closer together and lessened the inclination of the plane on which the figures are set, so that their minute characterizations are more legible. Docile horses are placed in various positions, soldiers in shining breastplates, and notables of the Florentine upper middle-class — barely disguised by some Orientalizing details. There is a little Moor dressed in lively stripes, and Domenico himself, kneeling on the right and pointing to a personage behind him, who is probably the donor. In the foreground are the crowns of the Magi, and around the base bearing the date of the painting are the sack and the flask, the usual symbols of the journey that preceded the Nativity. The decorated ruins of the portico give the narrative a tone of courtly dignity. In the background the story is broken up into different episodes: the shepherds on the rocky heights hearing the good news, the horsemen on the hills, and in the center the broad port of the lagoon.

PIETRO PERUGINO
Portrait of a Boy (circa 1480–1490)
Oil on panel; 14 1/2″ × 10 1/2″. Formerly thought to be Alessandro Braccesi, secretary of the Council of Ten of the Florentine Republic. From the Grand Ducal Wardrobe it was moved to the Uffizi in 1800.

DOMENICO GHIRLANDAIO
(DOMENICO BIGORDI)
Florence 1449. Panel and fresco painter, head of a very active workshop, he operated mainly in Florence. In 1481 and 1482 he was in Rome for the decoration of the Sistine Chapel. He died in Florence in 1494
Adoration of the Magi (dated 1487)
Tempera on panel (tondo); 67 3/4″ in diameter. It came to the Uffizi Gallery in 1780.

LUCA SIGNORELLI. *Madonna and Child.*

The rhythm of the tondo is complicated by the conjunction with the simulated reliefs in circular niches painted in grisaille. Within the composition, the Madonna and Child are incorporated in the round format only indirectly, by means of numerous, complicated, recurring torsions. In the background, the artist exploits the limited space to develop themes dear to Humanism: shepherds playing flutes, domestic animals grazing among the rocks, the remains of a past civilization fantastically re-evoked.

LUCA SIGNORELLI. *Holy Family.*

This is another round composition in which the artist reacted to Botticelli's contemporary work in the same format. St. Joseph's is forcibly compressed within the form of the panel, his powerful knees projecting towards the spectator, like the extended hand of the Child standing in the center. The Madonna bends her head, but the lower part of her body, sunk within the broadly defined planes of drapery, forces the circular scheme. The books and their pages are suspended in illusory foreshortening. There is no room for a landscape in this exaltation of plastic form, which is a prelude to the heroic synthesis of Michelangelo's *Doni Tondo.*

LUCA SIGNORELLI. *Crucifixion with the Magdalen.*

In old age, Signorelli often became academic, yet his pictorial language on more than one occasion still had the strength of better days. That is the

On the left:
LUCA SIGNORELLI
Cortona circa 1450. Panel and fresco painter, student of Piero della Francesca and friend of Perugino. Active mainly in Umbria, the Marches and Tuscany. Around 1497 he executed the decoration of the cloister in the Abbey of Monteoliveto; in 1499 that of the Chapel of S. Brizio in the Cathedral of Orvieto. He died in Cortona in 1523.
Madonna and Child (circa 1490)
Oil on panel; 67″ × 46 1/4″.
(the diameter of the inner tondo is 46 1/4″).
In the monochrome border, below the figure of Christ and the roundels with the two Prophets, is the inscription in Latin: "Behold the Lamb of God." According to Vasari it was commissioned by Lorenzo di Pierfrancesco and hung in the Villa di Castello. It came to the Uffizi Gallery in 1779.

Above:
LUCA SIGNORELLI
Holy Family (circa 1495)
Oil on panel (tondo); 48 3/4″ in diameter.
According to Vasari it was executed for the Palazzo dei Capitani di Parte Guelfa in Florence.

LUCA SIGNORELLI
Crucifixion with the Magdalen
(circa 1500–1505)
Oil on canvas; 8′2″ × 5′5 1/4″.
On the back there is a black pencil drawing of *St. Jerome in Penitence.*
It entered the Uffizi in 1919.

case with this Crucifixion. In the foreground everything is reduced to essentials: Christ livid, his loins covered with a striped cloth; the Magdalen attracts our glance with her sweeping gesture and the red mantle impeccably arranged on her knee. In the background on the left the artist dwells on a landscape perhaps taken from reality. The gorge crowned by a fortress vaguely recalls the peaks of the Furlo, near Urbino. On the right are shown the events following the Crucifixion: the descent from the cross and the mournful return along the flank of the hill, in the cold light of dusk. The work is rich in references to contemporary culture and dense in contrasts. It is somber and dramatic in the tangle of bodies around the cross in the deposition scene. In the foreground it is more static, lingering over details. The skull, which recalls Northern symbology, is probed by the light, and provides a macabre detail in the lizard peering into its toothless jaws.

LEONARDO DA VINCI. *Annunciation.*

Traditionally ascribed to Domenico Ghirlandaio, it was only attributed to Leonardo in 1869 and subsequently to Ridolfo Ghirlandaio and to Verrocchio. In fact the work is characterized by a partial acceptance of traditions and by innovations in interpretation, and thus it lends itself to conflicting readings, although it is today unanimously given to the young Leonardo. The perspective system, for example, has been constructed with great nonchalance. At the vanishing point (near the jagged mountain) there is a convergence from the right of a large number of diagonals marked by the profiles of the stone quoins, the step, the window and the top of the sarcophagus. From the left, however, there is only one such line, the one that marks the opening of the parapet. The plan of the composition is also asymmetrical. It is laid out with a double point of view on the right, where the figure of the Madonna is articulated in pyramidal form. Then it extends freely to the left, where the low wall counts not as an element of separation

LEONARDO DA VINCI
Vinci 1452. Painter, sculptor and architect, he also devoted himself to scientific speculation and research. Active mainly in Florence (1470–1482 and 1501–1506) and Milan, he left Italy in 1517 for France, where he was the guest of Francis I. He died at Amboise in 1519.
Annunciation (circa 1472)
Oil on panel; 3'5" × 7'1 1/2".
It came from the Convento di S. Bartolomeo at Monteoliveto and entered the Uffizi in 1867.
On the right: detail.

but as a link between the garden and the background. Here the possibility of having the angel correspond in rhythm to the Madonna was discarded, the figure being constructed on a system of variously oriented diagonals. Although the sarcophagus introduced as a support for the lectern is a homage to well-known examples used by Verrocchio and Desiderio da Settignano, its plastic consistency is annulled by the outpouring of claws, leaves and volutes. The misty city by the sea and the port dotted with ships are of a Northern type, and there is Flemish inspiration in the elaboration of the sumptuous draperies. But the minutely realistic effects that had come from Flanders are defiantly rejected in the fantastic flora of the lawn, which is full of luminous corollas and leaves flickering like flames. A work that poses problems, this painting expresses some of the most precocious and imperious statements of the master.

LEONARDO DA VINCI. *Adoration of the Magi.*

It is not difficult to understand why this work remained unfinished. The artist had been commissioned to execute a work for public devotion, with

LEONARDO DA VINCI
Adoration of the Magi (1481–1482)
Oil and bister on panel; 8'3/4" × 7'11 1/2".
Commissioned by the monks of S. Donato at Scopeto, it was not completed and when the artist departed for Milan he left it in the house of Amerigo Benci. Subsequently it was in Antonio de' Medici's collection, and in the 18th century it was placed in the Uffizi; after being temporarily transferred to the Villa di Castello it was definitively moved to the Gallery in 1794. The best-known drawings connected with the preparation of the work are preserved in the Uffizi, the Louvre, the Royal Library at Windsor Castle and the British Museum.
On the left: detail of the background with pillars, ruined arches, horsemen and other figures.

LORENZO DI CREDI
Florence 1455/1459. Student of Verrocchio
and fellow student of Leonardo, he worked
in Florence, where he died in 1537.
Venus (circa 1490)
Tempera (?) on canvas; 59 1/2″ × 27 1/2″.

LORENZO DI CREDI
Annunciation (circa 1490–1495)
Tempera and oil (?) on panel;
34 3/4″ × 28″.

religious and social functions. After thinking of alternatives and reworking the idea, he laid out a composition that did not respect the conventional terms. In the foreground group, instead of the customary joyful atmosphere, he produced one of amazement and dismay. In the background he strayed into fragmentary perspective research (the ruins), studies of motion (the horsemen) and naturalist themes (the trees). The execution had become transformed in the hands of the artist into an exhausting process of self-clarification. As such, he left it as soon as he felt that he had resolved the problems he had been studying; unfinished for the others, but exhausted for him. The "unfinished" in fact becomes an objective here, as a means of expression that allows one to see the infinite dynamics of the painter's ideas. In the dense vortex of the figures around the Madonna, the sacred scene takes on mystery and drama and becomes an evocation of man's fate, suggesting the fundamental problems of existence and the creation, of faith, doubt and awareness. Refracted light and a flexible dynamic tension connect the forms in the foreground with those further away, and with the sharp profiles of the stairs, the succession of arches and pillars and the convulsive movement of the men and horses. It is a system in which the perspective network is no longer rigid, and the 15th-century conception of space is replaced by a more open and fluid vision, one that takes in the life of the cosmos not only in its grandiose aspects but also in its intangible vibrations, its momentary and fleeting apparitions.

LORENZO DI CREDI. *Venus.*

The young woman with muscles and polished skin is hypothetically identified as Venus because of similarities to the classical prototype of the Modest Venus. She is placed on a plane whose slight inclination affects her stance, and the transparent scarf falling to the ground seems like a prop to stop her from swaying toward the left, and to keep her hip within bounds. Her torso bends in the opposite direction, winding within the spiral of fine veil up to the point where her hand rests upon her breast. There the path of the scarf is inverted, and its aim is to support the drooping shoulder, while her glance is again directed toward the right, in a last abrupt change which terminates the undulating development.

LORENZO DI CREDI. *Annunciation.*

This small composition is centered around the division of space and surfaces, and is a valuable document of the interior decoration of the period, which was often based on the use of inlaid, carved, painted or stucco-decorated wood. The subject is not so much an Annunciation, since Mary and the Angel are mute in their suspended attitudes, placed in two dead areas of the space. It is the room, which one enters by the step decorated with scenes from Genesis and which one leaves by the portico opening on a sunny landscape. This wooden box open toward the spectator extends to the right as far as the platform of the bed and the lectern, which are aligned to complete the perspective frame. Its openwork is arranged in an exact harmony, and the planes are scanned by pilasters and molded cornices. Equally balanced is the alternation of smooth surfaces and others decorated with rows of beading, palmettos and stylized tendrils and leaves, as well as classicizing figures judiciously borrowed from contemporary sculpture.

ÃNO SALVTIS M CCCCL...IXXXV DE XX FEBRVAR

FILIPPINO LIPPI
Prato, 1457. Student and assistant of Botticelli, he worked mainly in Florence. He was in Lucca around 1480 and in Rome between 1489 and 1493 (frescoes in the Carafa Chapel in S. Maria sopra Minerva). He died in Florence in 1504. *Madonna and Child with SS. John the Baptist, Victor, Bernard and Zenobius* (dated 1485; according to the Florentine style, 1486). Tempera on panel; 11'7 3/4" × 7'4 1/2".
The Latin inscription on the step in the foreground gives the date: 'AN(N)O SALUTIS MCCCCLXXXV DIE XX FEBRUAR ("20 February, year of Salvation 1485"). Executed for the Sala degli Otto di Pratica (today the Sala dei Duecento) in the Palazzo della Signoria.

FILIPPINO LIPPI. *Madonna and Child with SS. John the Baptist, Victor, Bernard and Zenobius.*

An altarpiece intended for the Chapel of S. Bernardo in the Palazzo della Signoria was ordered from Leonardo in 1478. He did not complete this work, nor did Ghirlandaio, to whom the commission was transferred some months afterwards. Although Lippi's altarpiece was painted eight years later, it includes a portrayal of St. Bernard and comes from the same palace. Consequently the hypothesis has been advanced by critics that Lippi utilized a panel that had already been prepared and sketched in by Leonardo, or at least employed one of his drawings. This is very likely, but it does not lessen the originality of the results achieved by Lippi. In particular, the two angels in the upper part, who are linked with garlands, the ribbons, the crown and the shell in a broad revolving movement, all derive from an idea of Leonardo's. Responsibly following out this suggestion,

FILIPPINO LIPPI
Allegory of Hate (circa 1485–1490)
Tempera on panel; 11 1/2" × 9".
Documented as being in the Grand Ducal Wardrobe at the beginning of the 18th century. It was moved from there to the Pitti Palace, and then to the Uffizi in 1919.

Lippi created a space open toward the exterior and a composition projected outside, relying on a double broken rhythm. Above, in the cornice, it marks the succession of pilasters and ends in the niche; and below it defines the stepped arrangement of the saints with respect to the podium on which the Madonna is seated. The vibrant mobility of the pleated robes, architectural passages, densely carved and gilded reliefs, show how precocious and acute were Lippi's observations of Leonardo's painting, which was also to provide him with new incentives for his future work.

FILIPPINO LIPPI. *Allegory of Hate.* *p. 87*

The artist has discarded the didactic aspects of the allegorical theme. It seems as if two brothers are playing in the grass and brush of a green-brown, gold-tinted meadow. The snakes elegantly unwinding their coils are compositionally linked by the Latin inscription flowing freely in air, which means: "There is no worse plague than family enmity." In the background the view opens on the buildings of Florence, somewhat veiled by mist, as if to suggest that the allegory might extend to include the turbulent city.

PIERO DI COSIMO. *Immaculate Conception.*

Often indifferent to sacred and liturgical conventions, which he sometimes subtly subverts, Piero di Cosimo found a stimulating point of departure in the theme of the Immaculate Conception. It is the flashing apparition of the Holy Ghost, which releases an exceptionally intense and limpid light. To develop it, the most anti-conformist painter in Florence of the late 15th century chose a symmetrical arrangement of figures as well as landscape, which rises in two steep grassy crags crowned with trees. On them are represented, as if taking place at the same time as the scene in the foreground, the *Nativity,* the *Annunciation to the Shepherds* and the *Flight into Egypt.* Leaving aside the quest for the dynamic, Piero has immobilized every element of the composition. He consolidated and burnished the pictorial materials, utilizing resonant passages of yellow, red, blue and brown to create figures that seem to be modeled in ivory and semiprecious stone, and trees that appear to be cut out of metal.

PIERO DI COSIMO
Florence 1462. Student of Cosimo Rosselli, but was more influenced by studying the paintings of Leonardo and Filippino Lippi. He always worked in Florence, devoting himself to easel painting as well as to decorative pieces for interiors, such as *cassoni.* He died in Florence in 1521.
Immaculate Conception (circa 1500)
Tempera and oil on panel; 7'11" × 5'7 1/2". The Madonna, with the Holy Ghost overhead, is surrounded by Saints Philip Benizzi, John the Evangelist, Peter and Antoninus standing, and Saints Catherine and Margaret kneeling. The predella has been lost. Painted for the Tebaldi Chapel in the church of the Servi (SS. Annunziata), in 1670 it passed into the collection of Cardinal Leopoldo de' Medici and subsequently to the Uffizi (1804).

MARIOTTO ALBERTINELLI. *Visitation.* *p. 90*

Mariotto Albertinelli's fame has been limited by his reputation as the collaborator of one of the greatest and most problematical painters of late 15th-century Florence: Fra Bartolomeo della Porta. Like Fra Bartolomeo, he was a rabid Penitent and belonged to the group of painters around the monastery of S. Marco, who were in Savonarola's confidence. Primarily, however, he shared his comrade's interest in Perugino's pictorial language, of which this Visitation, considered the artist's masterpiece, is one of the most enlightened instances. From this stems the coincidence with the style of Raphael's Florentine years, a coincidence that has been artificially complicated by scholars to the point of postulating an influence on Raphael by the two Florentine painters. It is unquestionable that the monumental size of the figures, their relationship with the architecture and the clear divisions

MARIOTTO ALBERTINELLI
Florence 1474 — Florence 1515
Visitation (1503)
Oil on panel; 7'8 1/2" × 4'11".
From the church of the Preti della Visitazione in S. Michele della Trombe. In 1786 it was sent by the Office of the Ecclesiastical Patrimony to the Accademia di Belle Arti, and was placed in the Uffizi. The predella with the *Visitation* is shown elsewhere in the same Gallery.

of the landscape, coincide with the example of Fra Bartolomeo. In their unexpected spatial immensity they show their difference from Perugino's world. And the unfolding of the narrative, enlivened by the profile of Elizabeth and the lateral set of the shoulder, typifies Albertinelli's inventiveness.

MICHELANGELO. *Holy Family*.

The symbolism of this painting is still being debated. Tolnay's reading seems accurate: the nude figures in the background represent humanity before the Law (that is, before God gave Moses the tablets) united through St. John to Mary and Joseph, symbol of humanity under the Law. The Child, looming over the two figures, represents humanity under Grace; He wears a headband, the ancient symbol of victory.

It is the only panel painting definitively attributable to Michelangelo that has come down to us. Executed in all likelihood after the *Pitti Tondo* (Na-

MICHELANGELO
Caprese 1475 — Rome 1564
Holy Family (1504–1505)
Tondo: resin and tempera on panel; 47 1/4" in diameter. According to evidence Anonimo Magliabechiano, the work was still in the Doni household between 1537 and 1542. In 1653 it is listed in an inventory of the Tribuna in the Uffizi. It was executed for the marriage of Agnolo Doni and Maddalena Strozzi, which took place at the beginning of 1505. Some scholars, however, set its date ahead to 1506 or to 1508–1510. The magnificent frame is by Domenico di Francesco del Tasso, and was probably designed by Michelangelo himself.

tional Museum, Florence) and the *Taddei Tondo* (Royal Academy, London), both of which are in marble, this work concludes or at least radically modifies the master's thinking in terms of circular composition. In comparison with the two sculptures, here an articulated relationship with the background (nudes and exedra) has been added. Two vanishing points control the composition. A lower one determines the perspective of the exedra, while a slightly higher one (indicated by the direction of the cross on St. John's shoulder) gathers the lines on which the main figures are set. This doubling, determined probably by the work's original position in the house of the Doni family, is made inconspicuous through the junction made by the step on which Joseph rests.

The lively relationship of the planes reinforces the twisting movement of the central group. Around this complicated structure revolves the band of the frame. In it the faces of the "witnesses" (prophets and sibyls), except the one above which is frontal, emphasize the perspective developments and revolve and descend in a repeated rotary movement, attracted by the figurative and symbolic core. As in the marble tondos, where the smooth surfaces of the foregrounds flowed into the "unfinished" backgrounds, to emphasize depth and distance, the resonant pictorial texture of the main group crumbles in the progressive blurring, from St. John to the nudes. In fact, in the foreground group itself the painting is denser on Mary's knees than on the face and head of St. Joseph. A work "typical" of the inquiring mind and genius of Michelangelo, it shines out at the beginning of the 16th century as an element of attraction and crisis for many personalities, great and less great, and then becomes a model for late 16th- and 17th-century pictorial programs.

GIORGIONE.   *The Trial of Moses.*

The rare subject of the picture is the trial by fire to which the child Moses is subjected (he is about to pick up the burning coal from the brasier) for having stepped on Pharaoh's crown.

Cavalcaselle's intuition, which in 1871 ascribed it to Giorgione, despite L. Venturi's initial negative attitude (1913), was generally accepted by the critics, who recognized the over-all conception, as well as the execution both of the landscape and of the central group of the woman and child with two youths, as Giorgione's. The other figures were considered to be by assistants. Here of course opinion is discordant, and attributions go from Campagnola (Fiocco) to "his colleague Master Catena" (Morassi) and to an unidentified Ferrarese (Longhi). It is fruitless to conjecture on the reason for such a collaboration, which in any case was not unusual with Giorgione. Certainly the central group is by far superior to the rest in its finesse of drawing and color, which have a specific Bellinian flavor. The most notable achievement, however, is the relationship between the figures and the open space in which distance is created by compositional devices (the screen of trees), virtuoso drawing (the wandering river, the road, the rolling hills), and by aerial perspective.

GIORGIONE
Castelfranco circa 1477 — Venice 1510
The Trial of Moses (circa 1505)
Panel; 35″ × 28 1/2″.
With the *Judgment of Solomon* in the same Gallery, which shows many affinities including size, it was listed in 1672 among the objects at Poggio Imperiale belonging to the Grand Duchess. In 1795 the two paintings entered the Uffizi, as works by Giovanni Bellini. Cavalcaselle was the first scholar to suggest the name of Giorgione.

93

LORENZO LOTTO. *Madonna and Child with Saints.*

Lotto composed this picture in Venice, where at the time — 1530 to 1540 — he was living permanently, if that may be said of this restless artist. Although it is only a year later than the poetic Holy Family in the Accademia Carrara, Bergamo, it appears more low-keyed in tone and more controlled in the forms of the drapery. We are at the beginning of the last phase of Lotto's career. Berenson was the only critic (1955) to read the composition attentively, noting the German motive of St. Anne sitting on a cushion and holding between her knees the Madonna, who presses the child to herself. The child is the formal and psychological center of the composition. It seems more fitting to read it as the sentiment of a solitary artist, without home or family, who creates this intimate image of daily life, with the whole family gathered around the lively child: the Madonna pressing against her mother, St. Joseph wrapped in thought, the old people enchanted and worshipful.

LORENZO LOTTO
Venice circa 1480 — Loreto 1556
Madonna and Child with Saints
(signed and dated 1538)
Canvas; 25 1/2" × 32 1/4".
The canvas entered the Uffizi in 1798, coming from the Grand Ducal Wardrobe.

RAPHAEL
Urbino 1483 — Rome 1520
Madonna of the Goldfinch
Oil on panel; 42" × 30 1/4".
Executed for Vincenzo Nasi, according to Vasari, it was badly damaged in the collapse of the Nasi houses in 1524. It was restored by Michele di Ridolfo del Ghirlandajo. From 1666 it belonged to the collection of Cardinal Carlo de' Medici, at the Uffizi. Critics almost unanimously agree that it was painted in 1506.

RAPHAEL. *Madonna of the Goldfinch.* p. 95

This is one of the most celebrated and perfect Madonnas of Raphael's Florentine period. To his work under Perugino and some influence from Piero della Francesca, he had recently added a lively interest in Leonardo's activity, which — besides the pyramidal structure — is more evident in works like the *Terranova Madonna.* The view around the group of figures is panoramic, and the variety of movements is noted serenely, transforming the joyous narrative into a tense abstraction. It is a coincidence of values in which one of the most original instances of Raphael's imagination is achieved. The crystalline abstraction makes the narrative clearer and at the same time exalts its most hidden emotions. The pyramidal knot of figures clarifies its own architectural nature precisely in the tension of the most subtle emotion. The landscape background fits in perfectly. It is the visible part of an exactly defined space that wheels around the figures. The background scenes are relaxed melodies, humanized Elysian fields where everyday scale, the affecting vision of a living and familiar countryside can be identified with an ideal model.

RAPHAEL. *Portrait of Leo X with Two Cardinals.*

This portrait is perhaps the masterpiece of the artist's last years, and certainly the work of this period most completely executed by his own hand, though the participation of Giulio Romano is documented. The "invention" is of the highest caliber. Note the structure of the central figure with its three-quarter turn in the armchair; the architectural plan of the two bodies at the side, like chapels built around a central apse; and the outpouring and the attraction of the red fullness of the table. The relationship of these elements, the abstraction of the calm surfaces, the intense expressions of the three men are the highlights of this painting. As if to accentuate further this golden ideal of space, the color extends without marked refractions, almost in a monochrome, and it takes an anonymous place around the "invention," as if to avoid altering its essential values.

SEBASTIANO DEL PIOMBO. *Death of Adonis.* p. 98

Agostino Chigi brought Sebastiano del Piombo to Rome in 1511 and put him to work painting in his villa, subsequently called the Farnesina, where Raphael and his team were working. But the eyes and heart of the artist were attracted by the world of forms that Michelangelo was unfolding on the ceiling of the Sistine Chapel. The *Death of Adonis* suggests the moment when Fra Sebastiano abandoned Venetian ideas for the more closed, plastic forms of Rome. In this significant work Sebastiano creates a group of three large sculptural nudes in an atmosphere that still owes much to Giorgione: a lagoon landscape with a poetic view of Venice from the island of San Giorgio. The sorrowing Venus at center seems to be controlling a stab of pain with her gesture, and the maids turn to silence the bearded Pan, who is playing the flute. In this great creation of the Venetian emigré, done dur-

RAPHAEL
Portrait of Leo X with Two Cardinals
(1517–1518)
Oil on panel; 60 1/2" × 46 3/4".
Since 1589 it has belonged to the Uffizi, although from 1799 to 1815 it was in Paris as part of the Napoleon's loot. The two Cardinals beside the Pope are Giulio de' Medici and Leone de' Rossi. The date of the painting is confirmed by the facts that Leone de' Rossi was elected Cardinal in 1517 and died in 1519. A copy made by Andrea del Sarto for Federico II of Mantua is now in the Museum of Capodimonte.

ing a phase of stylistic and spiritual instability, the most striking thing is the control of the colors. Psychologically they are well adapted to such tragic and dramatic events.

ANDREA DEL SARTO. *Madonna of the Harpies.*

One of the most famous 16th-century Italian paintings, this work has long been considered the prototype of Florentine "classicism." It skillfully combines Leonardo's "nuances," Raphael's "proportion" and Michelangelo's "monumentality." For this skilled balance, Andrea del Sarto merited Vasari's description as the "faultless painter." There is no question that programmatically it is Andrea's most ambitious work, and its complexity includes its iconography. With Michelangelo's *Doni Tondo,* it is perhaps one of the highest manifestations of a type of intellectualized religious feeling of Neo-Platonic derivation, characteristic of the Florentine cultural milieu even after Savonarola's reforms. Indeed it was painted immediately after an intense and dramatic experience of Michelangelo's work, and the painter moreover utilizes proportions and rhythms inspired by Alberti. The space, however, is monumentally vast, and the entire composition is based on an

SEBASTIANO DEL PIOMBO
(SEBASTIANO LUCIANI)
Venice (?) circa 1485 — Rome 1547
Death of Adonis
Canvas; 6'2 1/2" × 9'4".
From the legacy of Cardinal Leopoldo de' Medici. In an inventory of 1698, it is ascribed to Moretto. Morelli in 1890 assigned it to Sebastiano del Piombo, and with some dissent (D'Achiardi, Bernardini, Suter) the most authoritative scholars have recognized it as by Sebastiano's hand at the beginning of his Roman period.

ANDREA DEL SARTO
Florence 1487 — Florence 1531
Madonna of the Harpies (1517)
Oil on panel; 8'10 1/4" × 5'10".
Inscribed in Latin on the pedestal is the signature: AND. SAR. FLO. FAB. ("Andrea del Sarto, Florentine, made it") and below. AD SUMMU(M) REG(I)NS TRONU(M) DEFERTUR IN ALTUM MDXVII ("To the Queen raised to the highest throne." 1517). It was executed for the nuns of San Francesco in Via de' Pentolini; in 1685 it was acquired by Ferdinando de' Medici and placed in the Pitti Palace. In 1795 it was moved to the Tribuna of the Uffizi. There are many preparatory drawings in the Louvre and the Uffizi.
The book the Madonna holds with her hand is a symbol of wisdom, and the pedestal on which she stands is decorated with sphinxes (not harpies, as they are traditionally described) which are mythological symbols of the wisdom of Minerva. The accompanying figures are St. Francis (the Franciscan order first supported the dogma of the Immaculate Conception) and St. John the Evangelist, who was designated by the dying Christ as the adopted son of Mary, and in whose Gospel there is a reflection of the Neoplatonic mystique. The inscription is the beginning of a hymn celebrating Our Lady of the Assumption, Queen of Heaven and *sedes sapientiae* — the seat of wisdom.

unfaltering structure, in which the broadly shadowed, low-keyed colors give resonance to the spaces. Del Sarto achieved one of the most heroic attempts to redirect Florentine painting into the channel of its glorious 15th-century heritage. He felt it was necessary to do so in view of the intellectualistic deviations of the new Mannerist generations.

ANDREA DEL SARTO. *Portrait of the Artist's Stepdaughter.* p. 100
This is a disquieting work, one that foreshadows the intensity of Romanticism by playing on the ambiguous meaning of Petrarch's sonnet, "Go, warm desires," which is legible on the page of the open book. The circuit made by the arm takes us back from the page to the childishly ambiguous and pointed face, with its look of complicity. The light models the gorgeous opulence of the damask, with a lingering descriptiveness that will not be found in any other work by del Sarto. It is almost as if he wished to emphasize affectionately and ironically the formal clothes and ornaments of a girl who was very dear to him. Some reference to Raphael may be seen

in the relationship between the arms, the hands and the circuit of the arm-chair (see the *Portrait of Julius II,* which del Sarto could have seen during a trip to Rome in 1514). In any case, the largeness of the pose, the prominence it gains from the intensity of the color and the clear, resounding structure are among the greatest and most typical results of del Sarto's art.

ANDREA DEL SARTO. *St. Michael Weighing Souls.*
In the small, perfectly defined space, two figures light up with a flaming pictorial substance, and the shadows seem to come from an illusory darkening of the light itself, like ash forming on a burning coal. The free composition, and the dramatic surge balanced by the pairs of wings, are given dimension and repose by the rhythms and the architectural framework, which is subtly developed and illuminated with a sensitivity that seems to anticipate the refined effects of 17th-century interiors. The rapid touches and clots of the summary brush strokes — of the type often called "impres-

100

ANDREA DEL SARTO
Portrait of the Artist's Stepdaughter
(circa 1528)
Oil on panel; 34 1/4″ × 27 1/4″.
In the Tribuna from 1589 and attributed to Pontormo; this attribution was corrected in 1636.
The subject's features are those of Maria del Berettaio, daughter of Andrea's wife, Lucrezia del Fede, by her first husband, and after her mother the painter's favorite model. Inscribed on the book she holds are two complete sonnets by Petrarch: "Go, warm desires, to a cold heart" and "The earth, heaven and the elements witness."

sionistic" — create the refractions that are the source of the composition's dynamics. It is the prototype of a kind of painting commonly used in the second half of the 16th century and in the 17th century for predellas and sketches, which are often the freest and most novel works of artists who are otherwise rhetorical and academic.

ANDREA DEL SARTO
St. Michael Weighing Souls (1527)
Oil on panel; 8 1/4″ × 17″.
It is the first panel of the predella of the altarpiece with SS. Michael, John Gualbert, John the Baptist and Bernardo degli Uberti, which Andrea del Sarto painted for the church of the Romitorio delle Celle in Vallambrosa. Until recently exhibited in separate fragments at the Uffizi, the altarpiece has now been joined together. The other three sections of the predella are probably the work of students.

TITIAN. *Portrait of a Knight of Malta.* p. 102
The impress of Giorgione's spirituality is readily recognized in the idealized construction of this face, emphasized by the soft bands of the hair and the somewhat melancholy expression. So grandiose a layout for a portrait is not, however, imaginable before late in the second decade of the 16th century, thus its attribution to Giorgione cannot be accepted. Longhi's suggestion (1946) that it is probably a Paris Bordone is understandable, precisely because it displays an elegant interpretation of a Giorgionesque idea. But the structural force of the image, which generates space with the curve of the arm, and the pictorial quality of the white shirt developed through the play of the pleats against which the precious necklace stands out are

101

both typical qualities of Titian. After his personal success in the frescoes of the Scuola del Santo in Padua (1511), which in fact are a reaction to Giorgione, Titian on his return to Venice becomes the heir of Giorgione's poetic creativity. Scholars who confirm the attribution to Titian include Suida (1933), Morassi, Pallucchini (1952–1953) and Valcanover.

TITIAN. *Portrait of Eleonora Gonzaga.*
Della Porta wrote to Eleonora that, struck by the marvelous likeness of the portrait, "with difficulty I restrained myself from kissing the hand, so alive did it seem to me." The delicate ringed hand in fact seems ready to receive homage. The rich dress and the dignity of the pose create a division between us and the subject, who gives nothing of herself. The portrait was executed in Venice, as is known by a letter from the Duchess to her husband. One has the impression that Titian, obliged to concentrate on the

TITIAN
Pieve di Cadore circa 1488–1490
— Venice 1576
Portrait of a Knight of Malta
(circa 1515). Canvas; 31 1/2″ × 25 1/4″.
On the back an old inscription reads "Giorgio da Castelfranco called Giorgione." It belonged to the collection of Paolo del Sera, a Florentine noble residing in Venice, from whom Cardinal Leopoldo de' Medici bought it in 1654.

decorations of the dark dress, the rich jewels and the sophisticated hairdo, eyed the changing sky beyond the window and caught one of its melancholy aspects. He evoked it over a memory landscape, of the mountains of the countryside where he was born.

TITIAN. *Portrait of Bishop Ludovico Beccadelli.* *p. 104*
The portrait presents no problem of dating or subject. The subject appears to be immersed in a discreet shadow, which lightens toward the right. The face of the prelate, who fixes us with a firm look, is defined by the grey-brown of the background and the somewhat darker grey of his mantle. This subtle balance of the formal means of expression corresponds to the artist's intuition of the subject's reserved spirituality. Ludovico Beccadelli was in fact a subtle humanist, and also a participant in the far-reaching movement for religious revival led by Cardinal Contarini. He was mild, wise and far-seeing in exercising his function as intermediary between the Venetian Republic and the Holy See, just at the time when the Counter Reformation became harsher everywhere, in response to the directives of the Council of Trent.

TITIAN
Portrait of Eleonora Gonzaga
(1536–1537) Canvas; 45″ × 40 1/4″.
The portrait came to the ducal collection in 1631, with the Della Rovere legacy. A letter from the courtier Giovan Maria della Porta to the Duchess of Urbino states that the painting was already in Pesaro in April, 1538. It is a companion piece to the portrait of the subject's husband, Francesco Maria della Rovere, which is also in this Gallery.

TITIAN
Flora (circa 1515)
Canvas; 31″ × 24 3/4″
The painting came to the Uffizi through an exchange of pictures with Vienna, where it had gone with the collection of the Archduke Leopold William. The title comes from the engraving executed by G. Sandrart when the painting was in Amsterdam, in the collection of the Ambassador Don Alfonso Lopez. The engraver named the woman Flora after the flowers she is holding in her hand.

TITIAN
Portrait of
Bishop Ludovico Beccadelli (1552)
Canvas; 43 3/4″ × 38 3/4″.
Written in Latin on the paper the subject holds in his hand is the statement that Titian Vecelli painted the portrait of the 52-year-old Bishop, who was Apostolic Nuncio in Venice, in the month of July, during the reign of Pope Julius III. In a later hand it goes on to say that after September 18, 1555, Pope Paul IV transferred it to the Archbishop of Ragusa, who received it in the following December. The painting is mentioned in a letter and a sonnet by Aretino in the same year. It is not known who sold it to Cardinal Leopoldo de' Medici in 1673.

On Pages 106–107
TITIAN
Venus and Cupid (after 1555?)
Canvas; 3′11″ × 6′4 3/4″.
The painting came to the Uffizi in 1632 from the estate of Antonio de' Medici, but there is no mention in the documentary sources of the person who commissioned it.

TITIAN. *Flora.*

While Raphael was painting the Stanze in Rome for a world imbued with humanistic culture, Titian in Venice was reinterpreting Giorgione's classicism. He did this by creating fables of human life and love and composing his splendid variations on the theme of feminine beauty. The most famous of these is the so-called *Flora,* a sister to the nude seated on the sarcophagus in the Borghese Gallery painting. The composition is extremely simple. The body is seen in front view with the head in three quarters and slightly bent. While the young woman holds up the blouse slipping off her shoulder with her left hand, she bends her right arm and extends the hand full of flowers toward us, which gives the space a suggestion of depth, since the background is just a screen. A succession of softly curving lines encloses areas of clear color. A subtle chiaroscuro competes with the light to reveal the forms.

TITIAN. *Venus and Cupid.* *pp. 106–107*

Titian painted three pictures in which this image of a nude Venus appears, not exactly reclining but lying on her side on a bed hung with velvet, and turning her head toward an appealing cupid. In the versions in the Prado and the Kaiser Friedrich Museum, Berlin, the composition is embellished with a third and very important figure, an organ player who turns to look at the group, suggesting a narrative plot and emphasizing the esthetic and sensual tone. In this version, which Gronau, Berenson and Tietze consider to be entirely by the artist's own hand, there is a greater sense of serenity. The harmony of the beautiful woman remains intact, as she lies near a window opening onto a landscape seen as if through a heat haze. Pallucchini (1952–1953) accepts Berenson's suggestion that it was executed after 1555, and explains some stiffness in the purple mantle and in the modeling as the work of assistants.

TITIAN. *Venus of Urbino.*

Scholars generally agree in recognizing this famous painting as the one Vasari saw at Urbino and described as "a young recumbent Venus, surrounded by flowers and delicate draperies of great beauty." Comparison

TITIAN
Venus of Urbino (1538)
Canvas; 46 3/4″ × 65″.
It was commissioned by Guidobaldo della Rovere, Duke of Camerino and later Duke of Urbino, in 1538. In that year, in fact, the Duke sent an emissary, Girolamo Fantini, to Venice to collect his portrait and the "nude woman." It came to Florence in 1631 with the Della Rovere legacy.
Right: detail.

CORREGGIO
(ANTONIO ALLEGRI)
Correggio 1489 — Correggio 1534
Rest on the Flight into Egypt
Oil on canvas; 41 3/4″ × 48 1/2″.
It was in the Munari Chapel in the church of
San Francesco at Correggio. The Duke of
Modena removed it in 1649, replacing it
with a copy which is now in San Sebastiano.
In 1744 the Grand Duke of Tuscany re-
ceived it in exchange for Andrea del Sarto's
Sacrifice of Isaac, which is today in Dresden.

is inevitable with Giorgione's Venus in Dresden. Recollections of Giorgione seem to guide Titian's brush particularly in the fine definition of the
color and the glazing of the forms of the head and the white bedding.
Around 1540, of course, the painter had broadened his means of expression, and his pictorial sense corresponds to a more comprehensive and
sensual view of things. Thus we have here the spirited representation of
the two maids taking dresses out of the chest, the curled up dog and the
plants on the windowsill silhouetted against a darkening sky. It is all these
details, besides the knowing look of Venus's face, that creates the poetic
quality. A warm reality permeates it, in comparison with the subdued and
solemn air in which Giorgione's goddess sleeps.

CORREGGIO.   *Rest on the Flight into Egypt.*
Traditionally dated as belonging to the early maturity of the painter, this
work according to some recent studies was executed during the years between the decoration of the Camera di San Paolo in Parma and the cupola

110

CORREGGIO
Adoration of the Child (circa 1520)
Oil on canvas; 65 3/4″ × 32″.
In the inventory of the galleries, covering 1589 to 1634, it is reported that the painting was given to Cosimo II by the Duke of Mantua in 1617.

of the cathedral in the same city. In fact, both the conception derived from Mantegna — seen in many of the youthful works — and the Ferrarese influence from Francia, Costa and Dosso are surpassed in the harmony between the complex compositional balances and in the particular inflection of the light. Correggio reinterprets the lesson of Leonardo in a sort of intense evening tonality, which can lighten or emphasize the masses as the balance requires, and which provides accents of intense lyricism to a fabulous narrative.

CORREGGIO. *Adoration of the Child.*

Probably completed during the same years as the preceding work, this painting even more clearly reveals the characteristics of the master's maturity. This is so, despite the presence of architectural elements, which the overwhelming structure of light had eliminated in the Parma frescoes. The stepped relationship between figures, architecture and landscape is achieved in a play of luminous glazes that are both intense and fluttering, like the poised gesture of Mary.

JACOPO PONTORMO
(JACOPO CARUCCI)
Pontormo 1494 — Florence 1557
Supper at Emmaus (1525)
Oil on panel; 7′6 1/2″ × 5′9″.
It was painted in 1525 for the Foresteria
(guest house) of the Charterhouse of Gal-
luzzo, immediately after the fresco decoration of the cloister. Subsequently it went
to the Accademia, then to the Uffizi. The
Eye of God in the center is probably an
addition by Empoli, who also did a copy of
this work, with some variations.

JACOPO PONTORMO. *Supper at Emmaus.*

This work is perhaps the highest surviving expression of Jacopo Pontormo's so-called "Dürer moment," given the deplorable condition of the frescoes of the Passion which were painted at the same time for the same Charter-house. The rapid, rising perspective and the "Gothic" deformation of the figures are among the most evident results of Pontormo's interest in the German painter, which is also shown in the general iconography and in several descriptive passages. The strong centering of the rhythm on the roundness of the table, compressed by the edges of the picture, gives rise to a series of forms corresponding to one another, measured off in the same rhythm and incorporated in a dense perspective network. But here the device becomes the highest style as it is set against intense facial characterization.

JACOPO PONTORMO. *Portrait of a Woman with a Basket of Spindles.*

Among the masterpieces of Pontormo's portraiture, this is certainly one of the most problematical. If, as is thought, it was executed between 1517 and 1519, it would be contemporary with the great *Altarpiece of San Michele Visdomini,* which is considered his first fully mature work. In the altarpiece the stylistic and cultural coincidences with the work of the art-

JACOPO PONTORMO
*Portrait of a Woman with
a Basket of Spindles*
Oil on panel; 8′10 1/4″ × 5′10″.
Mentioned in the "Secret Archives of the
Pitti Palace" in 1773. Its provenance is
uncertain. In the 19th century,
scholars ascribed it variously
to Bacchiacca, Puligo and Andrea del
Sarto; now it is unanimously considered
one of Jacopo Pontormo's youthful
masterpieces. It is dated around 1518.

ROSSO FIORENTINO
Florence 1495 — Paris 1540
Moses Defending the Daughters of Jethro (1520–1523)
Oil on canvas; 63″ × 46″.
It may perhaps be identified with the work that Vasari states was painted by Rosso during his last stay in Florence, for Giovanni Bandini. It was bequeathed to the Uffizi by Don Antonio de' Medici in 1632.
Right: detail.

ist's master, Andrea del Sarto, seem to diminish and the restless and anti-conformist mind of the young painter turns to that anti-classical program which, according to some scholars, would be one of the most important turning points of his career. Without the *Portrait of Lucrezia del Fede* (about 1514), today in the Prado, and the *Portrait of a Sculptor* (1518) in London, which are of capital importance in the early maturity of Andrea del Sarto, it would be difficult to understand the present masterpiece. The revolving displacement of the planes to define a compact mass in movement is typical of del Sarto, and very different from the neo-Gothic, harshly heraldic stamp of the great portraits of Pontormo. However, the disquietude shown in the faces and in the combinations of color is indubitably an element of Pontormo's new style.

ROSSO FIORENTINO. *Moses Defending the Daughters of Jethro.*
Nineteenth-century critics considered this work to be a sketch, because of the lack of glazes on the color planes, which gives the "unfinished" look derived from Michelangelo (from the *Doni Tondo,* in particular), and

114

which is necessary for the separation and dramatization of the imposing masses. It is one of the masterpieces of Rosso's full maturity.

Michelangelo's influence is seen in the multiplication of the nudes and the application of the color, but Rosso's narrative hyperbole takes a highly original turn in the cut and structure of the composition. A violent impression of headlong and tumultuous drama is balanced by a calculated weighing of symmetry and perspective. The composition is based on clearly scaled planes, with neatly intersecting coordinates. The displacement of the vanishing point to the female figure on the right is redressed by its new centering (perhaps originally called for by the placing of the picture) on the opening of the legs in the central figure. The splendid female figure corresponds exactly to the dark nude on the left, completing a balanced effect. The special dramatic development of this work, as in all of Rosso's masterpieces, comes from this clear contrast between modular repetition, resolved in an instant blocking of the forms, and in the implicit violence. The forms can become desperately human, even though they are modeled on "antique" sources or recall Michelangelo's *terribilità*.

PARMIGIANINO
(FRANCESCO MAZZOLA)
Parma 1503 — Casalmaggiore 1540
Madonna with the Long Neck (1534–1540)
Oil on panel; 7'1 1/2" × 4'4".
Commissioned by Elena Bejardi, wife of Francesco Tagliaferri, on December 23, 1534, who paid 303 gold scudi for it. Vasari describes it as "imperfect," and in fact at some points the surface is unfinished (note the head of the Child). The posthumous inscription on the step to the right bears this out. The Latin words mean that Fate prevented the artist — F. Mazzola of Parma — from achieving his intentions. It remained in the church of the Servi in Parma until 1698, when it was acquired by Ferdinando de' Medici for the Grand Ducal collection at the Pitti Palace.

PARMIGIANINO
Madonna of St. Zacharias (circa 1530)
Oil on panel; 28 3/4" × 24 1/2".
According to documents it was painted in Bologna for Bonifazio Gozzadini, before 1533. Vasari, however, states that it was executed for Count Giorgio Manzuoli. Bonasone made an engraving of it in 1543. It appears in an inventory made in 1605 of the Tribuna of the Uffizi.

PARMIGIANINO. *Madonna with the Long Neck.*
Initially under the influence of Correggio, Parmigianino, after a sojourn in Rome (1525 to about 1527), reveals his own highly original interpretation of the complex cultural ferment started by Michelangelo and Raphael in that city. A friend and companion of Perin del Vaga and Rosso, Parmigianino nevertheless developed his own style, which could assume a new formal elegance. If this experience is already clear in the *St. Jerome Altarpiece,* now in London, this *Madonna,* painted ten years later, reveals the style as completely resolved in a new current of influence from Correggio's luminous dynamics. The *Madonna with the Long Neck* is the painter's most celebrated work. In composition it is rigorously abstract, made up of turned, linked and corresponding forms. The slim colonnade in the background creates a sort of illusionistic space, a wing placed to support the rising and turning of the main group. At the same time the complex perspective permits the inclusion of the little figure of St. Jerome.

PARMIGIANINO. *Madonna of St. Zacharias.*
With the *Madonna of the Rose,* in Dresden, this is the most characteristic expression of the artist's late Bolognese period. He had not yet achieved the mastery that some years later would lead to the *Madonna of the Long Neck.* This *Madonna,* however, shows how the artist, after a Roman sojourn, returns to reflect on Correggio's poetic creativity. It is from this source that are derived the warm chromatic tensions, with their almost monotone golden hue, which lends themselves to fabulous and visionary transformations. But Parmigianino's personal language cools the emotions of the mythical backdrops in an abstraction of chiseled forms. These are then dissolved in the relationship between the principal group and the great foreground with the saint turning and flashing his glance outward.

PARMIGIANINO. *Portrait of a Gentleman.*

Compared to the self-portrait in a convex mirror executed a few years earlier, this work is sober in composition. The "invention" is simple and intense in the regulation of the light and the application of the color; it abstracts the descriptive elements and emphasizes a psychological moment. All elements are balanced and are placed on vertical and parallel axes. In addition, the abstract iconology has led some scholars to believe that Parmigianino provided the ancestry for Bronzino's portraiture.

AGNOLO BRONZINO. *Portrait of a Youth with a Lute.*

Despite the fact that there are no documents — and no documents are likely to be found — for the dating of this masterpiece, it is clear that the work belongs to Bronzino's early efforts in portraiture, along with the *Martelli Portrait,* the *Youth with a Book* and the somewhat prior Panciatichi portraits. Besides, Vasari himself recounts that on his return from Pesaro (1523) Bronzino executed a series of portraits that were "extremely natural and done with incredible diligence . . ." Some scholars have attempted to establish a parallel between the portraiture of Bronzino and Parmigianino. Aside from certain cultural correspondences, the accentu-

PARMIGIANINO
Portrait of a Gentleman (1527–1528)
Oil on panel; 39 1/2″ × 27 1/2″.
Of unknown provenance, it entered the Gallery of Self-Portraits at the Uffizi at the end of the 17th century. Some authorities (Quintavalle) undervalue this work to the point of considering it an old copy, while others (Freedberg) consider it one of the best examples of the artist's style. The latter scholar also repeats the old hypothesis that the painting may be a self-portrait.

AGNOLO BRONZINO
(AGNOLO ALLORI)
Florence 1503 — Florence 1572
Portrait of a Youth with a Lute
(after 1532)
Oil on panel; 37″ × 31″.
Provenance is uncertain and there
are no documentary sources.

AGNOLO BRONZINO
Pietà
(before 1530?)
Oil on panel; 41 1/4″ × 39 1/2″.
Almost certainly to be identified with the
Pietà that Vasari says was painted by Bronzino for the church of S. Trinità. Some
critics have attributed it to Pontormo, but
it is certainly a youthful work by Bronzino.

ated revival of 15th-century models — in the manner of defining the environment, in the relationship of line and color and in the tension produced
by the subtle glazing of the color surfaces — is more characteristic of
Bronzino's own contribution.

AGNOLO BRONZINO.   *Pietà.*

There is an obvious descent from Pontormo in this work, but the painter's
imagination seems to be more attracted by the monumentality of Fra
Bartolomeo. The "nordic" iconography of Mary's head cover is not a reference to Dürer, through the intermediary of Pontormo, but a specific re-
course to motifs acquired from Andrea del Sarto. The burning color, which
is rare in Bronzino's work, suggests a contact with Sebastiano del Piombo.
This detail creates a doubt concerning the youthful date of the painting
that is agreed on by most scholars. Among the artist's religious paintings,
it is certainly the most moving, precisely because it avoids the dramatic
and representational apparatus of other works.

AGNOLO BRONZINO.   *Portrait of Bartolomeo Panciatichi.*   p. 120
Among all the portraits by Bronzino, here an interest in the Mannerist style
of Parmigianino appears most evident. But the complex architectonic   **119**

AGNOLO BRONZINO
Portrait of Bartolommeo Panciatichi
(circa 1540)
Oil on panel; 39 1/2″ × 32 1/4″.
Mentioned by Vasari, together with its companion piece, *Portrait of Lucrezia Pucci* (Panciatichi's wife), which is also in the Uffizi.

"score" of the background takes us back to Andrea del Sarto, and through him to the great masters of the 15th century. Thus it is also with the axial emphasis of the figure and the resonant quality of the colors that define this solemn and emblematic personage of the Tuscan court.

AGNOLO BRONZINO. *Eleonora of Toledo and Her Son Don Giovanni.* Perhaps less rhetorical than the other painting of Eleonora, in the Pinacoteca Sabauda, Turin, this splendid court portrait is one of Bronzino's highest achievements. The extraordinary descriptive treatment of the dress, which might appear to be a *tour-de-force,* acquires almost the significance of a sacred ceremonial in contrast with the lapis-lazuli background. It is a contrast emphasized by the fixity of the two ducal idols, which we find again only in some of the major portraits by Holbein.

AGNOLO BRONZINO
Eleonora of Toledo with her Son Don Giovanni (1545–1546)
Oil on panel; 45 1/4″ × 37 3/4″.
The picture is mentioned by Vasari, but traditionally the boy has been taken to be the youngest son of Eleonora and Cosimo, Don Garzia. It was at the Villa della Petraia, and from there it went to the Uffizi in 1798. The sumptuous dress worn by the Duchess was probably her wedding gown; when her tomb was opened in 1857 it was found that she had been buried in the same dress.

JACOPO TINTORETTO. *Leda and the Swan.*

Pittaluga places this work late in Tintoretto's career, and judges it to have been executed with assistance, an idea accepted by Berenson and Tietze (1947). A comparison with a youthful version of the subject, with the figure of Leda alone, her body luminous and resilient, helps the argument. That version, formerly in the Contini-Bonacossi collection, is now in Palazzo Vecchio. The Uffizi version of the subject is noble and skillful in composition, with its play between the two contrapuntal figures and the imposing architecture of the female body, which recalls Tintoretto's somewhat academic *Mythologies* of the Palazzo Ducale in Venice. But there is a certain heaviness in the definition of the forms and a uniformity in the substance of the color.

JACOPO TINTORETTO. *Portrait of Jacopo Sansovino.*

Jacopo Tintoretto's portraiture has not yet been systematically distinguished from that of his son, Domenico, and by some scholars these por-

JACOPO TINTORETTO
Venice 1518 — Venice 1594
Leda and the Swan (circa 1570–1575)
5'3 3/4" × 7'1 3/4".
The work was in Cardinal Mazarin's collection, then the Duc D'Orleans', until 1798. It was bought by the Duke of Bridgewater, and subsequently came into the possession of Mr. Arthur de Noè Walker, who gave it to the Uffizi Gallery in 1893.

JACOPO TINTORETTO
Portrait of Jacopo Sansovino
(circa 1566)
Canvas; 27 1/2″ × 25 1/2″.
Since Borghini mentions it as being in Florence in 1584, the assumption is that it was sent there in 1566, when Sansovino was named a member of the Florentine Academy. Hadeln held that it was a studio work; there are other versions of the painting, which Tietze considered copies of this one. agreeing with Berenson that this alone is by the master's hand.

traits are doubted when compared with the highest creations of imagination. In fact, it must be recognized that his feeling for humanity helped him mainly in sounding the depths of the faces of the old. It is enough to recall the *Jacopo Soranzo* in the Castello Sforzesco, Milan, or the *Alvise Cornaro* of the Pitti, and their dematerialized and visionary effect. The portrait of the 80-year-old Sansovino, however, is the image of an artist who is still fully active (he displays the implements of his profession) and whose shrewd glance seems to be fixing his friend, Tintoretto, as he is in the process of painting him. From the letter of Calmo, we know that there was a strong friendship and mutual respect between the two artists.

PAOLO VERONESE. *Annunciation.* *pp. 124–125*
In the museum of Padua there is a precedent for this *Annunciation,* in a version showing a wide separation of the two figures of the angel and the

Virgin. Since the 18th century, scholars have vacillated between ascribing the authorship to Veronese or to Giuseppe Porta, called Salviati. This shows how readily the work may be seen in a Mannerist key, especially the angel, with his complicated and violent gesture.

If, as seems reasonable, the Paduan work was done in 1552, this reprise of the motive in the Uffizi canvas may be four or five years later, and is still reminiscent of the *Coronation of the Virgin* in the sacristy of San Barnaba (an association suggested by Pallucchini). The impression of greater distension is conveyed mainly by the structural composition, which is spread horizontally and marked by the caesuras created by the white columns and the doorway opening on a tree-lined avenue. It is a theme that Veronese will take up again in his *Annunciation* of the Accademia, Venice, a work of his late maturity. Here the rich, gay color is shot with nervous yellow highlights, as if reflected from the light bursting from the glory of the angels.

PAOLO VERONESE. *Holy Family with Two Saints.*

The composition must have been bigger at one time. In its present form it has a closed-in rhythm, which is not usual in Veronese, who excelled in bal-

PAOLO VERONESE
Verona 1528 — Venice 1588
Annunciation
Canvas; 6′4″ × 9′6 1/2″.
Originally in the Venetian collection of Paolo del Sera, it was taken to Florence and acquired in 1654 by Cardinal Leopoldo de' Medici, as a work of Veronese. Subsequently it was assigned to Zelotti, to the school of Veronese, to the studio of Zelotti, and finally restored to Veronese, an attribution followed by the majority of critics.

ancing figures and effects of space. Yet Veronese's authorship of the painting is not disputed. It is admirable in the force of its plastic structure, which lends itself to a harmonious and elegant play of tender, human gestures. These are not an ostentatious display of virtuosity, but are functional devices conveying the feelings called for by the narrative. Particularly apt is the foreshortening of Joseph and St. John in the lower right-hand corner. The only virtuoso note is in the cascade of St. Barbara's golden hair and in the Oriental richness of her gold-striped silk dress. Scholars do not agree on the dating, some ascribing it to the artist's youthful period (Fiocco), others to the late period (Savini). It seems that the latter view is more acceptable and that the work may be associated with the famous altarpiece formerly in the church of Santa Caterina and now in the Accademia, Venice. The tone is deeper, but the richness of color, the consistency of the pictorial material and the affinity with the Accademia painting, establish the case. There is general agreement that the painting in Venice should be dated between 1570 and 1575. The work must have been popular in the 18th century, as the Guardi brothers were commissioned to copy it. Their version is now in the Seattle Museum (Kress Foundation).

PAOLO VERONESE
Holy Family with Two Saints
(1570–1575)
Canvas; 34″ × 48″.
The work is mentioned by Ridolfi (1648) as being in the Vidman household in Venice. Subsequently it belonged to the Venetian collection of Paolo del Sera, a Tuscan. It was then bought (1654) by Cardinal Leopoldo de' Medici, and entered the Grand Duke's collection in Florence.

PAOLO VERONESE. *Martyrdom of St. Justina.*

The work is not unanimously attributed to Veronese by modern scholars (Arslan assigns it to Carletto), and some doubt is suggested by Salvini, the author of a catalogue of the Uffizi (1956). Fiocco considers it a masterpiece of Veronese's youth. Even if one is inclined to consider it a contemporary copy, it was certainly made from a youthful work by Veronese's own hand. The insertion of the architectural element is inopportune, but the orchestration of the colors is interesting, in the live red of the drapery of the figure on the right, in the watered fabric of the saint's dress and in the luminous silk sleeves from which her trembling hands emerge.

PAOLO VERONESE
Martyrdom of St. Justina
Canvas; 40 1/2″ × 44 1/2″.
A small devotional picture, it is not the model for the *St. Justina Altarpiece* in Padua. It belonged to the Venetian collection of Paolo del Sera, was acquired by Cardinal Leopoldo de' Medici in 1654 and so came to Florence.

GIOVANNI BATTISTA MORONI. *Portrait of a Knight.*

If the earliest portrait by Moroni is dated 1547, in his Brescian period — which lasted until 1553 — the painter did a notable amount of portraiture, acquiring a clientele extending well beyond his provincial milieu. His ability to record reality, which comes from a direct Lombard influence, is untroubled by the pressures of Mannerist taste, though he takes account of them. They reach him through Venetian painting, on the margins of which he operates. The figure of the knight in his black suit, with the little Spanish ruff that had been in style for only a few years, stands out vividly in a space that would be almost abstract, if not for the perspective of the pavement and the base supporting the urn. The flame, the inscription and the languorous gesture convey a flavor of simple romanticism, in a somewhat meditative and eccentric taste. Beyond the window is a luminous townscape, as in certain backgrounds by the Lombard painter, Bergognone.

CARAVAGGIO. *Youthful Bacchus.*   *p. 128*

Although its quality casts doubt on Bellori's assertion that it was the painter's first work, it is certain that with *Ailing Bacchus, Boy Bitten by a Lizard* and *Boy Peeling a Pear* (known through copies) this painting belongs to the earliest phase of Caravaggio's career.

Compared to the other canvases mentioned above, which are close to it in the relationship between figure and still-life, this *Bacchus* has a greater balance in the closed passages of color, solidly defined in tense, resonant fields, within strong linear demarcations. The classical pose and the subtle calculation of the composition go well beyond the equivocal "realism" that is too often attributed to Caravaggio. This cannot be reconciled with the portrayal of forms in the splendid still-life.

In this formal perfection, which is certainly unusual in a very young artist and partially justifies those scholars who prefer a later dating, the torpid expression of the face is barely accentuated by the tilt of the head (with a very slight relaxation of the features that may recall Michelangelo's youthful *Bacchus*). It is perhaps the only element providing an immediate emotional contact with the spectator.

CARAVAGGIO. *The Sacrifice of Abraham.*   *p. 129*

In comparison to *Bacchus*, this *Sacrifice* shows the same concentration of light that already in the youthful works defines the space and the relationship between the figures, and that will have so much importance in Caravaggio's maturity. The rapid fanning out and down of the figures is developed from the angel's face to Isaac's, which blocks the dynamics of the main compositional lines with the tension of the head and the hand, and with the

GIOVANNI BATTISTA MORONI
Albino (Bergamo) 1523(?) — Albino 1578
Portrait of a Knight (1563)
Canvas; 72″ × 40 1/4″.
From the Grand Ducal Wardrobe, it came to the Uffizi in 1707. Below the Latin inscription on the column at left is the date MDLXIII and the signature "Io. Bap. Moronus p." The figure of the knight has been identified with Count Pietro Secco Suardo.

CARAVAGGIO
(MICHELANGIOLO MERISI)
Caravaggio 1573 — Porto Ercole 1610
The Sacrifice of Abraham (1591?)
Oil on canvas; 41″ × 33 1/2″.
Formerly in the Sciarra collection, it was
given to the Uffizi in 1917 by John Murray.
According to Bellori it was executed for
Cardinal Maffeo Barberini. Published in
1922 by Marangoni as an old copy from
Caravaggio, it is now recognized by almost
all scholars as an original work by the
painter.

CARAVAGGIO
Youthful Bacchus (circa 1589)
Oil on canvas; 36 1/2″ × 33 1/2″.
Published by Marangoni, following a sug-
gestion by Longhi, in 1917 as a copy after
Caravaggio, and by the same scholar in 1922
as an original. It was in the Uffizi reserves.
Probably it is the *Bacchus* that Bellori in-
dicates as the first work by the master.

"terrible" foreground. In clear contrast to the intense drama of the figures is the opening of the background and its calm isolation from the main group (unusual in Caravaggio's work).

GIUSEPPE MARIA CRESPI. *Massacre of the Innocents.* p. 130
The Uffizi possesses a print by Crespi on the same theme, but developed in completely different episodes. A certain Don Antonio Silva commissioned the subject, and Crespi devoted himself wholeheartedly to the task of carry-ing it out. The artist who began with the exuberant frescoes of Palazzo Pepoli and was asked by the Grand Duke of Tuscany to supply "mainly pleasing and popular little pictures," perhaps would not himself have chosen such a subject. Although by 1708 Crespi already had his own pictorial vocabulary, derived from the tradition of the Carracci and Guercino and spiced with influences from the spirited fancies of Mazzoni and Burrini, the unusual theme of the *Massacre* required another kind of force. Some ex-

amples of Magnasco's dark early manner perhaps suggested the tangle of bodies built up of geometric interconnections. The deep tone of the painting cannot be explained simply by the presence of a priming coat of Armenian clay. The material is thick and oily. Different and characteristic is Crespi's mannered style of dealing with physiognomy. It is most polished in the scene of the two disconsolate mothers, where the silvery tonalities of the color are also most beautiful. The drama finishes in Arcadia, with the flight of blithe little souls.

GIAMBATTISTA TIEPOLO. *The Erection of the Statue of an Emperor.* The work has been known since the first decade of the century, and Sack, who was the first to publish it, already mentions its bad state of preservation.

GIUSEPPE MARIA CRESPI
Bologna 1664 — Bologna 1741
Massacre of the Innocents (1708)
Canvas; 6'1 1/4" × 4'4 1/4".
The canvas was discovered by Marangoni in the Villa of Poggio Imperiale in 1920 and brought into the Gallery. According to the documentary evidence of Zanotti and the painter's son, Luigi, it had been given by Crespi himself to Prince Ferdinando of Tuscany, who became his fervent admirer.

GIAMBATTISTA TIEPOLO
Venice 1696 — Madrid 1770
*The Erection of the Statue of
an Emperor* (1734–1735)
Canvas; 13'9 1/4" × 5'9 1/4".
The work came to the Uffizi in 1900 from
the Seminario Arcivescovile of Udine. From
a payment recorded there it can be dated
between 1734 and 1735. Morassi (1962)
ascribed it to Menescardi. At the exhibition
in Udine (1966) Rizzi again proposed giving
the authorship to Tiepolo, but Morassi is
still doubtful.

131

Perhaps this is the reason for some hesitation, based on the deterioration of the paint, as to its authenticity. In conception, however, it is typical of Tiepolo. In the upper part, the Angel of Fame is a precursor of Truth in the Tiepolo ceiling in the museum of Vicenza, while the figures below are boldly foreshortened and arranged in stepped sequence. The proud soldiers are taken from the repertory already assembled in the Dolfin canvases, and in contrast is the appealing figure of light tonalities on the left.

FRANCESCO GUARDI. *Village with Canal.*
The motive of a natural or man-made arch that spans the actual space of a canvas and helps evoke a space in nature, reaches the 18th-century view painters from a 17th-century tradition. Francesco Guardi included it in his repertory of subjects, having certainly acquired it through Marco Ricci and Canaletto. Nor should we forget the almost obsessive examples offered by reality to anyone, like Guardi, who constantly traveled by boat along the Venetian canals.

But this imaginary view seems to stem less from a descriptive intention than from a musical inspiration: the repeated sequence of the arch and the counterpoint of light and shade between the banks. The material of the color is drenched in discreet light. The brush smoothly describes the groups of little figures and the ragged banner, which barely stirs in the quiet air.

FRANCESCO GUARDI
Venice 1712 — Venice 1793
Village with Canal (1765–1770)
Canvas; 11 3/4″ × 21″.
With its companion piece, which shows an *Arch and an Esplanade,* it was acquired by the Gallery in 1905.

**FLANDERS
GERMANY
HOLLAND
FRANCE**

ROGIER VAN DER WEYDEN. *Entombment.*

This is one of van der Weyden's masterpieces, and was executed during his brief stay in Italy in 1449. It is obvious that Rogier is not interested in narration. In fact, where Italian Renaissance painters like Raphael and Titian put the cortège transporting Christ into the scene or represent the moment when Jesus is lowered into the tomb, the Flemish painter avoids external drama and concentrates his attention on the nude and tortured body. Rogier's devotional intention is not to represent a given moment in the Passion, but to offer the lacerated image of Christ as an object of piety and adoration. The figures are thin and wavering, almost lacking in weight. To a certain extent, the painter is returning to the stylizations of the Gothic tradition, which Jan van Eyck had surpassed in the name of a more humanistic naturalism. In van der Weyden's panel, the importance given to the landscape may occasion surprise, as the painter, in contrast to van Eyck, often considered nature as a disturbing element, and in his great *Descent from the Cross* in the Prado he had set his figures against a gold ground. It is likely, however, that the inclusion of the broad landscape in the *Entombment* was specifically requested by the Italians who commissioned the work. Indeed, for the Italian admirers of the "new discipline from Flanders" an essential aspect of the Lowlands' pictorial miracle was the landscape passages evoking so subtly a sense of airy spaces. The symmetry and the Renaissance grandeur of van der Weyden's composition are probably the result of a study of Italian art. The problem of the influences experienced and exercised by the artist on the Italian peninsula has not yet been adequately investigated.

HANS MEMLING. *Portrait of a Young Man.*

Like the landscape, the portrait is a great discovery of the so-called "Flemish primitives." From the occasional efforts of Jan van Eyck to the numerous examples by Memling, it is possible to follow the evolution of Flemish portraiture. Van Eyck is rigorously, sometimes pitilessly, objective, and sets his subjects against dark grounds, so as to concentrate all the attention on their impassive faces. Van der Weyden utilizes a neutral ground and relies primarily on his sensitive linear quality. Petrus Christus, a student of problems in perspective, introduces foreshortened views of rooms and windows into his backgrounds. In Memling the novelty consists in luminous backdrops against which he sets his images, and in this he will have a large following, even in Italy. The portrait no longer interests Memling as a cold reproduction of the individual features. On his best portraits, Memling confers an elegiac tone that makes them works of subtle poetry. Numerous members of the golden youth of Bruges were portrayed by Memling, and often — as in this panel — they belonged to the Italian colony in that city.

ROGIER VAN DER WEYDEN
Tournai circa 1398. Worked with Robert Campin at Tournai under the name of Roger de la Pasture; from 1435 in Brussels under the Flemish version of his name: Rogier van der Weyden. In Italy (Ferrara and Rome) in 1449 and 1450. Died in Brussels in 1464.
Entombment (1449)
Oil on panel; 43 1/4″ × 37 3/4″.
Ciriaco d'Ancona saw it on August 8, 1449 and described it and its wings (*Adam and Eve Driven from Paradise* and *Portrait of Lionello d'Este*). It was also described by Bartolomeo Facio in his *De Viris Illustribus* (circa 1456).

HANS MEMLING
Seligenstadt circa 1435–1440. He worked with Rogier van der Weyden in Brussels around 1460–1464; after 1465 he was in Bruges, where he died in 1494.
Portrait of a Young Man
Oil on panel; 14 1/2″ × 10 1/4″.

HANS MEMLING
The Portinari Diptych
Oil on panel. The left hand panel, representing *St. Benedict* measures 17″ × 12 1/4″; the right hand panel, with *Benedetto Portinari*, 17″ × 12 1/2″.

HANS MEMLING. *The Portinari Diptych.*

The two small panels form a diptych. However, the figure of the young man at prayer suggests the Madonna and Child rather than a saint for the companion image, and it is supposed that originally there was a central panel representing the Virgin and the Infant Jesus. This panel is probably to be identified with the *Madonna and Child* of the Berlin Museum. The little triptych formerly belonged to the Ospedale di S. Maria Nuova in Florence. The *St. Benedict* and the *Portrait* entered the Uffizi in 1825; the *Madonna and Child* was acquired by Berlin from a private source in 1862. The identification of the young man with Benedetto Portinari was made by Warburg, and is based on the one hand on the presence of the saint of the same name, and on the other on the fact that the Portinari family had strong connections with the Ospedale di S. Maria Nuova. Benedetto Portinari was born in 1466 and thus was 21 years old when he was portrayed by Memling.

MASTER OF THE BARONCELLI PORTRAITS. *Portrait of Pierantonio Bandini Baroncelli and His Wife Maria Bonciani.*

These two portraits are another document of the deep interest in Flemish painting held by Tuscan bankers established at Bruges. Baroncelli became the agent for the Medici bank at Bruges in 1480, succeeding Tommaso Portinari. In 1478 Mary of Burgundy had named him her Gentleman of the Chamber and Duke Francis of Brittany his Keeper of the Household. In the documents his name is twisted into Piro Bonndin. In 1489 the Emperor Maximilian turned to him for a loan of 12,000 florins. The two portraits in the Uffizi were probably executed in 1489, the year in which Pierantonio married Maria Bonciani. The panels are evidently the wings of a triptych, whose central panel (with a *Madonna*) has been lost. A comparison with contemporary works by Memling shows that the images of the Master of the Baronelli Portraits are more trite, more stylized and closer to the firm style of Petrus Christus.

MASTER OF THE
BARONCELLI PORTRAITS
Anonymous painter active in Bruges around 1470–1490, who is so called from the two portraits mentioned below. He was a follower of Petrus Christus.
Portrait of Pierantonio Bandini Baroncelli and His Wife Maria Bonciani.
Oil on panel; 21 1/2″ × 13″ each.
On the backs of the panels an *Annunciation* is painted.

HUGO VAN DER GOES. *Portinari Triptych.*   *pp. 138–140*

This altarpiece is unique in 15th-century Flemish painting because of its imposing size. Van der Goes received the commission from Tommaso Portinari, who had been general agent of the Medici family in Bruges since 1465. In the left-hand wing, the painter portrayed Portinari with his sons, Antonio and Pigello, and in the right-hand one Portinari's wife, Maria Baroncelli, and their daughter Maria. As we know that Antonio was born in 1472, Pigello in 1474 and Maria probably in 1471, by estimating the ages of the children as they are shown in the painting it is possible to date it between 1476 and 1478.

The striking feature of the central panel with the *Adoration of the Shepherds* is the particular conception of the space. The ordinary observer is disconcerted by the fact that the group of shepherds which is supposed to be behind the angels is practically in the same plane with them. In reality, van der Goes's composition is derived from "sacred representations" in the

HUGO VAN DER GOES
Ghent circa 1440. In 1467 he became a Master at Ghent, where he worked until 1475; subsequently he was in the monastery of Roode Klooster, near Brussels, until his death in 1482.

Portinari Triptych (1476–1478)
Central panel:
Adoration of the Shepherds
Outside of wings: *Annunciation*
Oil on panel; 8'3 1/2" × 9'11 3/4", the central panel, 8'3 1/2" × 4'7 1/2", the wings.

theater. In these the various actors took their places on a stage that rose progressively toward the back. It is thus a "stage space," as Salvini has written. The theatrical character is further evidenced in the intense expression of the figures, and particularly in the ecstatic adoration of the angels and the exalted attitude of the shepherds. The figures are vigorously modeled. The faces reveal an irregular "beauty," which in the splendid features of the three shepherds achieves a realism that is completely new in Flemish painting. The still life in the foreground has always been much admired, with good reason. The flowers in the two vases — irises, lilies, columbine and violets — are symbols of Mary. What is striking in the two wings is the scale and dignity of the four saints. No less impressive are the portraits of the donors, with their strongly marked contours, the pallid coloration and intensity of expression. The landscape in the right-hand wing is also extraordinary. The large bare trees are worthy of Breughel. It is in this interweaving of realistic accents and visionary, atmosphere that the fascination of the great triptych lies. From its arrival in Florence in 1478 it has always aroused interest and amazement, on the **139**

one hand for its intensely naturalistic details, and on the other for the highly original modeling, which comes very close to tonal painting. Artists like Lorenzo di Credi and Piero di Cosimo borrowed many suggestions for their work from this panel. The *Portinari Altarpiece* remained in the church of S. Maria Nuova until 1897.

NICOLAS FROMENT. *The Lazarus Triptych.*
A highly important document of French Provençal painting in the latter half of the 15th century, it includes influences from the North and from the South. In Froment's triptych, the Flemish element is the strongest. The realism of the figures, the sensitive landscape and the interior inspired by Flémalle (in the right-hand wing), all point toward the Low Lands. Some **140** of the types are so close to Dirck Bouts as to suggest that Froment may

HUGO VAN DER GOES
Portinari Triptych (1476–1478)
Inside of left-hand wing: *SS. Thomas and Anthony Abbot with Tommaso Portinari and his Sons Antonio and Pigello.*
Inside of right-hand wing: *SS. Mary Magdalen and Margaret with Maria Baroncelli Portinari and her Daughter Maria.*
Each wing, 8'3 1/2″ × 4'7 1/2″.

have been trained in that artist's studio at Louvain. Aside from this, influences from Catalonia add a Mediterranean air. Although it had been preserved from time immemorial in the church of the Bosco ai Frati at Mugello, it could not have been painted there, as it has nothing to do with Italian art.

NICOLAS FROMENT
Uzès (Languedoc) circa 1430 (?). He may have worked with Dirk Bouts at Louvain before 1460; in 1465 he was at Uzès, in 1470 at Aix-en-Provence, and from 1472 at Avignon. He died in Avignon (?) around 1485.
The Lazarus Triptych
Oil on panel. Central panel, *Resurrection of Lazarus:* 69″ × 52 3/4″.
Left-hand wing, inside: *Christ and Martha;* outside, *Madonna and Child:* 69″ × 30″.
Right-hand wing, inside: *The Magdalen Pouring Unguents on the Feet of Christ;* outside, *The Donors;* 69″ × 30″.
Signed and dated May 18, 1461.

GERARD DAVID. *Adoration of the Magi.* p. 142

Because it is a tempera on canvas, this work has an historic interest. It is, furthermore, one of the best but least known works of Gerard David, and was executed by the artist in his youth, probably around 1490. A sensitive introvert, David avoided dramatic effects and experiments in form. He sums up rather, and terminates, the 15th-century tradition of Bruges. David often touches on poetry in the sense of the intimacy that he creates in his compositions, in which the figures are wrapped in silence and concentra- **141**

GERARD DAVID
Oudewater (Holland) circa 1450–1460. In
1484 he became a Master at Bruges, where
he then worked; in 1515 he was also Master
at Antwerp. He died in Bruges in 1523.
Adoration of the Magi
Tempera on canvas; 37 1/2″ × 31 1/2″.

tion, and psychologically isolated from one another. In Gerard David's
paintings unity is achieved also by means of the color and by the diffused
golden light.

MASTER OF THE VIRGO INTER VIRGINES. *Crucifixion.*

One of the three largest studios operating in Holland at the end of the 15th
century was that of the Master of the Virgo inter Virgines, the other two
being those of Geertgen tot Sint Jans and Hieronymus Bosch. The work
that gives the anonymous master his name is the panel representing the
Virgin and Child and Four Holy Women in the Rijksmuseum, Amsterdam.
The artist is notable for the charge he is able to give his works, anticipating

MASTER OF THE
VIRGO INTER VIRGINES
According to Friedländer he was active in
Delft around 1480–1495.
Crucifixion
Oil on panel; 22 1/2″ × 18 1/2″.

142

the so-called "Antwerp Mannerists" of the early 16th century. In the *Crucifixion,* note the highly expressive motive of the fainting Madonna, with her body collapsing in on itself, or the figure of the Magdalen at the foot of the cross, with her trunk bent back and her hair wildly disheveled. It is a kind of painting that is far from Gerard David, who was also Dutch, but very different in temperament.

ALBRECHT DÜRER.　*Adoration of the Magi.*

This famous painting fuses various aspects of Dürer's art. It shows his taste for chiseled images with continuously vibrant contours, as well as

144

ALBRECHT DÜRER
Nuremberg 1471. In 1486 he was working with Michael Wolgemut; in 1492–1494 he was at Colmar, Basel, Strasburg and in 1494–1495 in Venice, Padua and Mantua. In 1505–1506 he went to Venice and Bologna; in 1520–1521 he was in the Low Countries. He died in Nuremberg in 1528.
Adoration of the Magi
Oil on panel; 39 1/2″ × 45″.
Monogrammed and dated 1504. The wings are in Frankfurt and Munich.

ALBRECHT DÜRER
Madonna and Child
Oil on panel; 17″ × 12 1/4″.
Monogrammed and dated 1526

his thorough study of perspective. Again, there is his psychological unity and tension in narration and strong feeling for landscape, which is more compact and organic than in the Flemish painters. The work also testifies to the tension, ever present in Dürer, between theory (which the artist termed *Kunst*) and manual ability (*Brauch*). The *Adoration of the Magi* is the central panel of the *Jabachsen Altarpiece*. Its two wings are in Frankfurt and Munich.

ALBRECHT DÜRER. *Madonna and Child*.
It is one of the master's late works, and comes at the end of his tireless career, which had taken him from one end of Europe to the other. The 145

ALBRECHT DÜRER
St. Philip and *St. James*
Oil on panel; 17 3/4″ × 15″ and
18″ × 14 1/2″ respectively.
Monogrammed and dated 1516.

rounded 16th-century-type forms are sculptural and solidly occupy the space. The painter is fond of laying out a complicated play of curves, which is evident here down to the small arms and hands of the Infant Jesus. The problem of proportions and the definition of beauty had always concerned Dürer, who wrote three works on theory. Where the Italians theorized on the "absolute," Dürer defended "relative" beauty. "When I was young," he said, "I went mad over variety and novelty. Now, at my advanced age, I have learned to admire nature's innate reserve and to understand that this simplicity is the ultimate aim of art."

ALBRECHT DÜRER.   *St. Philip* and *St. James*.

The two heads are "engraved" with an extraordinary precision and subtlety of line, corresponding to the spur of a tormenting morality. It suggests the tense moment in which the Reformation is about to break out in Germany. Dürer's two saints clearly share this climate. Note the burning eyes of Philip and James, their bitterly grimacing mouths and the long curling beards. Dürer was a man of his time and passionately concerned with the spiritual problems being debated around him. He immediately sided with Luther, as he states in several powerful passages in the *Reisebuch* (Travel Journal) he kept during his stay in the Low Lands (1520–1521).

ALBRECHT DÜRER.   *Portrait of the Artist's Father*.

A youthful work, executed when he was 19, this portrait shows that Dürer had already formed a style and possessed an unmistakable pictorial lan-

ALBRECHT DÜRER
Portrait of the Artist's Father
Oil on panel; 18 1/2″ × 15 1/2″.
Monogrammed and dated 1490.

guage. The influence of Flemish models is apparent, but Dürer goes beyond the portrait conceived as a document. His images are connected with life, history and the tensions and aspirations of his subjects. Behind the sensitive linear scheme in the *Portrait of the Artist's Father,* it is possible to read this desire on the part of the painter to state the character, the firmness and strength of will, as well as the fineness of mind of his parent.

LUCAS CRANACH THE ELDER. *Adam* and *Eve.*

What a contrast there is between the severe, rational and Renaissance art of Dürer and the playful, decorative art of Cranach. Whereas Dürer is preoccupied with the problem of the proportions of the human body (both in his paintings and his graphic work there is considerable evidence of these intensive studies), Cranach's nudes are free of any preconceptions or even observation of "anatomical correctness." Naturally it would be a waste of words to state that in art this is perfectly legitimate. Cranach's nudes (Eve, Venus, Diana, Judith, Lucrece) are slender, elongated, flexible, boneless and often affected in their poses. A cold, refined eroticism is exuded. Often the figures are set against dark grounds that throw the silhouettes into relief and highlight the flesh of the bodies. Cranach repeatedly painted the figures of Adam and Eve against a dark background. He also placed them in front of impressively painted, stylized foliage. Finally, he showed them in the Earthly Paradise, surrounded by animals. Cranach's art still presents problems concerning the definition of his style and the clarification of its relationship with Italian and Flemish art.

ALBRECHT ALTDORFER. Two Scenes from *The Life of St. Florian*
pp. 150–151

With some of the other great works of the 16th century, including those of Italians like Lotto, the fantastic, visionary and fabulous art of Albrecht Altdorfer represents the other side of the Renaissance medal: the irrational. In this area are the individuals on the fringe, the enemies of classical ideology and of all doctrinaire baggage. It is not surprising, then, that official criticism at one time could view Altdorfer with a sense of indulgence, and could consider his art as an uncultivated manifestation of an instinctive and elementary temperament, which it was better to ignore. If today we can appreciate Altdorfer's painting, this is due to our education in modern taste and to our familiarity with the fantastic and surrealist currents in contemporary art. In fact, Albrecht Altdorfer's art may be termed "surrealist," inasmuch as it appears to be tied to a world of dreams. As in a dream, the images in Altdorfer acquire the colors of the rainbow, the narrative becomes exciting and frightening, distances grow short or stretch into infinity. All this may be observed in the two superb scenes from *The Life of St. Florian,* where in the marvelous orchestration of colors, the unforgettable whites stand out with a snowy purity. The Uffizi panels are part

148

LUCAS CRANACH THE ELDER
Kronach (Northern Franconia) 1472. In 1503 he was in Vienna; from 1505 to 1550 at Wittenberg as painter to the Court of Saxony. He traveled in the Low Countries in 1508. In 1550 he was at Augsburg. He died at Weimar in 1553.
Adam and *Eve*
Oil on panel; 67 3/4" × 24 3/4" and 65 3/4" × 24" respectively.
The *Adam* is monogrammed and dated 1528.

ALBRECHT ALTDORFER
Ratisbon (?) circa 1480. Active at Ratisbon (Regensburg), of which he became a citizen in 1506. In 1535 he traveled to Vienna. He died in Ratisbon in 1583.
Departure of St. Florian (above left)
Martyrdom of St. Florian (opposite)
Oil on panel; 32" × 27 1/4" and 30" × 26 1/4" respectively.

of a polytych that the Bavarian artist probably painted for the church of St. Florian near Linz. It made a grandiose ensemble, whose numerous parts were unfortunately dismembered and scattered. Seven of the panels have been recovered, but it is possible that some others have been lost.

HANS SÜSS VON KULMBACH
Kulmbach near Bayreuth (?) circa 1480. Before 1503 he worked with Jacopo de' Barbari. In 1511 he became a citizen of Nuremberg. He died at Nuremberg in 1522.
St. Peter Walking on the Waters (above right) (from the *Altarpiece of SS. Peter and Paul*)
Oil on panel; 50 3/4" × 37 3/4".

HANS SÜSS VON KULMBACH.   *St. Peter Walking on the Waters.*
This scene is part of a large *Altarpiece of SS. Peter and Paul,* an imposing composition made up of eight large panels. Ten scenes are represented. Besides the figures of St. Peter and St. Paul on the backs of the wings, which are visible when they are closed, the artist has depicted: *St. Peter Walking on the Waters, Deliverance of St. Peter, St. Paul in Ecstasy, Decollation of St. Paul, Preaching of St. Peter, Calling of St. Paul, Martyrdom of St. Peter, Parting of St. Peter and St. Paul.* Süss von Kulmbach, who died prematurely in 1522, at Nuremberg, was the master of a decorous art flanking that of his older colleague, Dürer, whose studious approach and acute graphic sensitivity he shared. Von Kulmbach was certainly not

151

PETER PAUL RUBENS
Siegen (Westphalia) 1577. Worked with
Tobias Verhaecht, Adam van Noort and
Octavius Vaenius in Antwerp; Master at
Antwerp in 1598; in Italy and Spain 1600–
1608; at Antwerp from 1609, but made
journeys to Holland, Paris, London, Madrid
(1628), etc. He died at Antwerp in 1640.
Isabella Brant (circa 1625)
Oil on canvas; 33 3/4″ × 24 1/2″.

equipped to follow Dürer in all his interests. More conservative, he and
his pupils inherit the traditions of Michel Wolgemut's studio, where Dürer
himself had served his apprenticeship. The provenance of the Uffizi's *Altar-piece of SS. Peter and Paul* is unknown. Nor is there any certainty about
the composition's dating, which is generally accepted to be about 1510.

PETER PAUL RUBENS. *Isabella Brant.*
Isabella Brant was Rubens' first wife; he married her in 1609, when he re-turned to Antwerp after his journey to Italy. She was an intelligent and sen-sitive woman, and Rubens lived happily with her until her death in 1626.
Rubens' portraits are intended to exalt the physical and psychic energy of his
subjects in a single, generous, vital impetus. It is exactly this vital quality
that saves the highly cultivated Rubens from academic coldness. A robustly
naturalistic feeling — translated into an extraordinary flexible technique
combining Flemish and Venetian practice — is masterfully expressed in
this portrait.

PETER PAUL RUBENS
Henry IV at the Battle of Ivry
Oil on canvas; 12'5" × 22'8".
Work in progress from 1628 to 1631,
but unfinished.

PETER PAUL RUBENS. *Henry IV at the Battle of Ivry.*

In 1622 Marie de' Medici had commissioned Rubens to do two large series of pictures for the decoration of the Palais du Luxembourg, which had just been built. The first series of canvases — twenty-two in all — was completed by the painter in February, 1625 (it is now in the Louvre). Immediately afterwards, Rubens started to work on the second cycle, which was to represent episodes in the life of Henry IV, Marie de' Medici's husband, who had been assassinated in 1610. The project was not completed, however, because of dissension between Marie de' Medici and her son, Louis XIII, and her subsequent departure for the Low Countries. As shown by the inventory of Rubens' possessions made after his death, the master had started on six of the very large canvases. Two of these have come down to us: the one reproduced here and a second, also in the Uffizi, representing the *Triumphal Entry of Henry IV into Paris after the Battle of Ivry.* Preparatory sketches for some of the compositions have also been preserved. The two gigantic canvases in the Uffizi are in an incomplete state, and it is this that makes them so interesting. In *Henry IV at the Battle of Ivry* the influence of the great Italian models (Leonardo's *Battle of Anghiari,* Giulio Romano), is clear, but the impetus with which the artist has attacked his theme is entirely new and Baroque.

JOHANN LISS. *Venus at Her Toilette.*

German by birth, Liss was a cosmopolitan European artist, in training and spirit. After studying, from 1616 to 1618, in the most active centers of Netherlandish art (Haarlem, Amsterdam and Antwerp), he completed his education in Rome and Venice, and died prematurely in the latter city in 1630. The style of Liss's painting is Baroque in a minor key. The artist avoids the bombast of "official" art and pursues the quality of grace — the grace that will triumph in the succeeding century. Above all, Liss is an exquisite colorist, with a soft and sensual touch.

HERCULES SEGHERS. *Rocky Landscape.*

Various currents may be distinguished in 17th-century Dutch landscape painting. Among them are a naturalistic vein — having nature, whether Dutch, Italian, Scandinavian, etc., as subject — and a visionary vein, of which Hercules Seghers (along with Jakob van Geel) is one of the great exponents. Joos de Momper's Mannerist art is at the basis of Segher's landscape painting, but the example is softened, made vivid and tragic. Segher's landscapes, impressive in the mysterious play of light and shade, are mirages of the soul, the highly subjective visions of an artist who gave himself to solitude, in pursuit of his inner genius. In a certain sense, the painter was a kindred soul to Rembrandt, who owned a number of Segher's paintings, including this one.

ANTHONY VAN DYCK. *Jan Van Montfort.* p. 156

The restless and elegiac van Dyck distinguished himself primarily, as is well known, in the field of portraiture. In the early 17th century he gave ideal

155

ANTHONY VAN DYCK
Antwerp 1599. In 1609 working with Hendrick van Balen in Antwerp; Master at Antwerp in 1618; in 1620 in London; in Italy from 1621 to 1627 (Genoa, Florence, Venice, Rome, Palermo, etc.); Antwerp from 1627 to 1632; at The Hague in 1632; in London from 1622 to 1640; in Paris in 1641. He died in London in 1641.
Jan van Monfort
Oil on canvas; 48″ × 35″.

interpretation to a large part of the European aristocracy, conveying not only their exterior pomp but also the refinement of their style of living. In Rubens, it has been said, "the men are like lions and the women like domestic animals: strong, healthy and beautiful beings, but not human figures with a spiritual individuality" (Friedländer). This observation could never be applied to van Dyck, who aims rather to spiritualize and exalt his clients. The present portrait "is certainly one of the most vigorous by van Dyck, in the sureness of the organization of the forms and the color, which make up the translation of the subject's arrogant air of self-confidence into pictorial terms" (Salvini).

REMBRANDT VAN RIJN
Leyden 1606. With Pieter Lastman in Amsterdam; worked there from 1632. He died in Amsterdam in 1669.
Portrait of the Artist as a Young Man
(circa 1634)
Oil on panel; 24″ × 20 1/2″.

REMBRANDT VAN RIJN. *Portrait of the Artist as a Young Man.*

p. 157

The gallery of self-portraits by Rembrandt is surely one of the most impressive in the history of art and recalls that of another great Dutchman, van Gogh. Rembrandt's self-portraits differ from one another greatly in pose, chiaroscuro and psychological content. The painter, especially in his youth, enjoys painting himself dressed up in fantastic costumes, as is evident in the present work. This taste for masquerade (a Baroque characteristic) interests Rembrandt because of the great possibilities it offers for new and unexpected pictorial effects. Note, in fact, in our *Portrait of the Artist as a Young Man* the splendid glow of light that the painter knows how to create in the metal collar and the chain on top of it. The glow is mysterious, as there is no clear source of the light that strikes the figure, leaving it partially veiled in shadow. It is this anti-naturalistic light that molds and reveals the figure, which takes shape without traditional contour lines. This *Portrait of the Artist* is dated about 1634.

158

Above:
REMBRANDT VAN RIJN
Portrait of the Artist as an Old Man
(circa 1664)
Oil on canvas; 27 1/2″ × 21 3/4″.

On the left:
REMBRANDT VAN RIJN
Portrait of an Old Man
Oil on canvas; 40 1/4″ × 28 3/4″.
Signed; date illegible.
According to Zwarts (*Oud Holland,* 1926) it is the Rabbi Haham Saul Levy Morteyra of the Portuguese community in Amsterdam. It should be dated perhaps around 1658.

REMBRANDT VAN RIJN. *Portrait of an Old Man.*

Rembrandt's art should be seen in the historical context of middle-class Amsterdam society, which was certainly the most advanced society in Europe at the time. Thanks to this privileged position, Rembrandt was able to free himself without external difficulty of the mythical superstructures which were so much a part of the work of that great man of the world, Rubens. Rembrandt's independent attitude grew in intensity in his late years, when the artist increasingly left behind conventions, employing thick impasto and a short-hand technique. The present portrait, probably of an Amsterdam rabbi, is dated about 1658.

REMBRANDT VAN RIJN. *Portrait of the Artist as an Old Man.*

The self-portraits of Rembrandt as an old man are among the most extraordinary of all his works. Before his own face, the painter loses the restraint that he might have felt in dealing with another person's features, and he expresses his need for introspection and for truth. Two of the most impressive self-portraits of Rembrandt in old age are those of Aix-en-Provence (a painfully contorted portrayal) and of Cologne (tragic mask of an old man laughing), but the present canvas is just as significant. Here the artist gives himself the appearance of a grand personage of the Renaissance (Rosenberg). Yet the hollow eyes, the bitter contraction of the mouth and the summarily painted costume give the picture a mournful and anti-heroic character. The Uffizi possesses a third self-portrait by Rembrandt, which was executed around 1655.

JEAN BAPTISTE SIMÉON CHARDIN. *Girl with Shuttlecock.*

p. 160

Chardin started as a still-life painter, but soon he was also devoting himself to the composition of scenes of family life, with the same sensitivity for luminous "clotted" colors, skillfully juxtaposed. It has been pointed out that Chardin's genre scenes are conceived like still-lifes. In fact, they are devoid of any sense of movement, and the painter shows complete indifference to anecdote. The points of departure that 17th-century Dutch art could offer are transformed in delightfully intimate compositions, made up of the pictorial values of dense and broadly-applied color, and of strong, clearly defined form. "His manner of painting is singular," writes Bachaumont. "He places one color next to the other, without mixing them, so that his works somewhat resemble mosaics, like the type of needlework called cross-stitch." And in Diderot's view: "It is difficult to understand this sort of magic. Thick layers of color seem to ooze into each other. Elsewhere, one would say that they were a mist or light froth blown on to the canvas. . . . Go up close and everything gets confused, flattens out, disappears; go back a ways and it is all built up again." With his love for humble things and the simple life of the lower middle-class, Chardin found himself in clear opposition both to the Rococo and the new Neo-Classicism. Certainly he was the most "modern" painter of his century in France. The Uffizi also possesses a magnificent companion piece to the present canvas, *Boy Playing Cards*. Both paintings were acquired by the Gallery in 1951.

HISTORY OF THE MUSEUM
AND ITS BUILDING

GIORGIO VASARI
Uffizi Gallery
External View
Photo Alinari

HISTORY OF THE COLLECTIONS

The building that houses the Uffizi Gallery was erected by order of Cosimo I de' Medici, as the offices (hence "Uffizi") of the State Judiciary.

The idea of changing the use of the structure, whose appearance was more showy than ministerial, and turning it into an art gallery came from Cosimo's son, Francesco I. He had already had the same architect, Vasari, construct his famous Studiolo in the Palazzo Vecchio, and now he was expanding his plans as collector and connoisseur, in keeping with the humanistic vocation that had been for ages the root of the Medici family's interest in the arts. It is well known that Lorenzo the Magnificent had collected in the gardens of S. Marco, where the Accademia still stands, a large number of ancient marble sculptures, for study by young artists, and that Michelangelo received his early training there. Beginning with Cosimo the Elder, the Dukes and then the Grand Dukes of Tuscany had in fact grasped the prestige value of possessing such collections, and the continual effort to increase them had its political side. The rooms now housing the Medici collections were designed by Buontalenti, in accordance with a rather ostentatious conception of museum display, in which the works of art were treated as part of the interior decoration. The Gallery was ready for visitors in 1581.

Since that time the Uffizi has aroused the enthusiasm of writers, scholars and artists, including early visitors from Bocchi (1591) to Pigafetta (1600). The Gallery represented a complete cross-section of Mannerist thought and art, beginning with the decoration of the walls, with frescoes by Alessandro Allori and his assistants. It occupied the east wing, on the first floor of which the Teatro Mediceo (the space now occupied by the print and drawing collection) was built in 1585; two years earlier a roof garden had been laid out on top of the Loggia dei Lanzi. In the west wing were the workshops of the Grand Dukes' gold- and silversmiths, master craftsmen in porcelain, mosaic, semiprecious stones, etc.

The Grand Duke Ferdinand II, with his brother Cardinal Leopoldo, practically doubled the size of the gallery by taking over the workshops for the display of new acquisitions, around the middle of the 17th century. Thus the east gallery was now connected by a U-turn running above the riverside portico to a corresponding west gallery, whose rooms were decorated by a troop of local artists with a series of paintings celebrating the glories of Tuscany. Cardinal Leopoldo was responsible for the Gallery of Self-Portraits, later arranged in Vasari's Corridor between the Uffizi and the Pitti Palace. With the enlargement of the Gallery the collection was correspondingly increased.

Almost every work exhibited at the Uffizi has its own particular story. The weak and ailing Cosimo II enriched it with Correggio's *Holy Fam-*

ily, which had been given to him by the Duke of Mantua. From the estate of Don Antonio de' Medici came Mantegna's *Triptych,* and in 1631 on the extinction of the sovereign family of Urbino, whose heir was the Grand Duchess Vittoria, the two portraits by Piero della Francesca, Raphael's *Self-Portrait* and a group of works by Titian: *Venus of Urbino* and the two portraits of the duke and duchess. By 1635, Michelangelo's *Holy Family* was already hanging in the Tribuna. In 1639, Correggio's *Rest on the Flight into Egypt* was obtained by an exchange with the Duke of Modena. Even Cosimo III, who succeeded Ferdinando II in 1670, despite his questionable role on the political level, seems to have been a true benefactor of the Gallery, and it is likely that he was responsible for the acquisition of one of Rembrandt's greatest masterpieces, *Portrait of Rabbi Morteyra,* and of Leonardo's *Adoration of the Magi.* Meanwhile his son, Ferdinando, was stripping churches and convents of works of art for his collection, which on his death in 1713 also went into the Gallery. One of these was Andrea del Sarto's *Madonna of the Harpies.* And on the death of Giangastone, when the Medici dynasty came to an end, an act of enlightened munificence marked its close. The sister of the last Grand Duke, Anna Maria Luisa, who had married the Elector Palatine, drew up an agreement with the new ruler, Francesco III of Lorraine, later confirmed in her will (1743), which bequeathed all of the Medici collection to the person of the prince, but "on the express condition that it is as an ornament of the State, for the utility of the public and to attract the curiosity of foreigners, and that none of it shall be removed or taken out of the Capital and the State of the Grand Duchy." Thus what is considered to be one of the greatest collections in the world became the inalienable heritage of Florence.

With the House of Lorraine, in particular under Francesco III and Pietro Leopoldo, the organization of the Gallery underwent a revision in the spirit of the Enlightenment, thanks to the new classification of the material by "schools," which was introduced after 1780 by Luigi Lanza. Interest was concentrated on the paintings, and much of the other material was removed from the Gallery and placed elsewhere. This period is still marked by very important accessions, like those obtained through exchanges with Viennese museums, such as Titian's *Flora,* Giovanni Bellini's *Allegory* and Dürer's *Adoration of the Magi.* During the Napoleonic era various works left the Gallery, among them the ancient marble sculpture called the *Medici Venus,* which was later returned. In the course of the 19th century, the establishment of different branch museums around the city made it possible to decentralize the immense collection, which had been increased at the end of the century by the acquisition of the Arcispedale di S. Maria Nuova's picture gallery. Early in the 20th century, Corrado Ricci, who was then the director, set up the print and drawing collection (Gabinetto dei Disegni e delle Stampe), which has more than 100,000 items and is equipped with exhibition rooms, a library and a photographic archive. After the repair of war damage, which was not very extensive, and the fortunate recovery of the masterpieces looted by the Germans, the main problems of the Uffizi concerned management and above all museum organization and display. Accordingly, during the 1950s, there were some memorable attempts at innovation, such as the impressive arrangement designed for Cimabue's *Christ* by the architects, Carlo Scarpa and Franco Albini. (The work was subsequently taken back by its owners, the Franciscan monks of S. Croce; it was poorly displayed in their refectory and then almost completely destroyed in the 1966 flood.)

Planning is now under way for a general rearrangement of the Uffizi, which calls for the removal of the State Archives (housed on the ground floor) and the utilization of the vacated space to help exhibit the collections more adequately. The church of S. Pier Scheraggio is also to be restored, and the offices of the Soprintendenza and its library, now in Vasari's building, are to be moved elsewhere. Vasari's Corridor to the Pitti Palace will be reopened and there will be a new link with the International Museum of Contemporary Art, now being established. The whole will make up an ample, well-defined museum organization, perhaps like no other in the world.

THE BUILDING

The building that now houses the Uffizi Gallery was constructed by order of Cosimo I de' Medici in order to bring together the thirteen principal magistratures of the State, whose offices had to be in the vicinity of Palazzo Vecchio, which was his residence. In 1546 demolition started in the thickly built-up area, and a street was opened between Arnolfo's Palazzo Vecchio and the Arno, destroying in part the church of S. Pier Scheraggio (the remains of which are visible in the Via della Ninna and in the ticket office of the Gallery) and the Zecca ("Mint") which stood opposite. Vasari was asked to draw up plans in 1559, and in the following year he notes in his memoirs that building had started on the Zecca side. Because of Cosimo's afterthought of including a corridor to link Palazzo Vecchio with the Pitti Palace, construction went on for much longer than anticipated, and in 1574, when Cosimo and Vasari himself died, it was still in progress. Alfonso Parigi and Bernardo Buontalenti (the creator of the bizarre doorway called the Porta delle Suppliche) who were commissioned to complete the job did not alter the original conception. This was based on a strict multiple reprise of Michelangelo's architectural motives on the Capitoline, combined with some suggestions taken from Mannerist architects ranging from Peruzzi to Vignola.

Vasari's inventiveness lies less in the decorative elements and the stylistic features of his deliberately toned-down architectural design, than in his plan seen as an urban design. In this he reveals an extreme sensitivity in inserting the gigantic complex of the Uffizi into the ancient center of Florence, without destroying its delicate fabric of history. By having his building turn to make symmetrical wings on either side of the Via dei Magistrati, he created a spyglass which instead of emphasizing its own value enhances the two farthest views, of Palazzo Vecchio on one side, and the green hill of the Costa di S. Giorgio on the other. Working with a structure made up of light membering and transparent effects, Vasari created a town-planning solution that is astonishingly modern.

A VESTIBULE
D FIRST GALLERY
1 SALA DELL'ERMAFRODITE (statue of the *Hermaphrodite*, Roman copy of a Hellenistic original)
2 13TH-CENTURY AND GIOTTO ROOM
3 14TH-CENTURY SIENESE ROOM
4 14TH-CENTURY FLORENTINE ROOM
5 AND 6 INTERNATIONAL GOTHIC ROOM
7 EARLY 15TH-CENTURY FLORENTINE ROOM
8 LIPPI AND POLLAIOLO ROOM
9 PIERO DEL POLLAIOLO ROOM
10, 11 BOTTICELLI ROOMS
12 FLEMISH ROOM
13 FLORENTINE ROOM
14 VAN DER GOES ROOM
15 UMBRIAN AND LEONARDO ROOM
16 SALA DELLE CARTE GEOGRAFICHE (Leonardo's *Annunciation*)
17 UMBRIAN ROOM
18 TRIBUNA (ancient statuary and portraits by Pontormo, Bronzino, Vasari, etc.)

19 PERUGINO AND FRANCIA ROOM
20 MANTEGNA AND DÜRER ROOM
21 GIOVANNI BELLINI AND GIORGIONE ROOM
22 HOLBEIN AND ALTDORFER ROOM
23 CORREGGIO ROOM
24 CABINET OF MINIATURES
E SECOND GALLERY (classical sculpture)
F THIRD GALLERY (classical sculpture and tapestries)
G VASARI'S CORRIDOR (temporary display of part of the collection of self-portraits)
25 RAPHAEL AND MICHELANGELO ROOM
26 ANDREA DEL SARTO ROOM
27 PONTORMO ROOM
28 TITIAN ROOM
29 PARMIGIANINO ROOM
30 EMILIAN ROOM
31 DOSSO DOSSI ROOM
32 SEBASTIANO DEL PIOMBO ROOM
33 CORRIDOIO DEL '500 (works by Vasari, Bronzino, Allori, etc.)
34 VERONESE ROOM
35 TINTORETTO AND BAROQUE ROOM

41 RUBENS ROOM
42 SALA DELLA NIOBE (*Niobe and her Children*, Roman copy of a Hellenistic original; works by Watteau, Nattier, Chardin, Longhi, Guardi, etc.)
44 17TH-CENTURY ROOM (Caravaggio, Rembrandt, etc.)
45 17TH- AND 18TH-CENTURY ROOM

Rooms 36 to 40 have been closed to permit the construction of a new exit staircase. Their exhibits are being temporarily shown in Rooms 42, 44 and 45. The numbering and designation of the rooms are the official ones employed by the Gallery. As a connection between the Uffizi Gallery and the Pitti Palace by means of the corridor across Ponte Vecchio is planned, readers are cautioned that the positions of some works may be changed in the next several years.

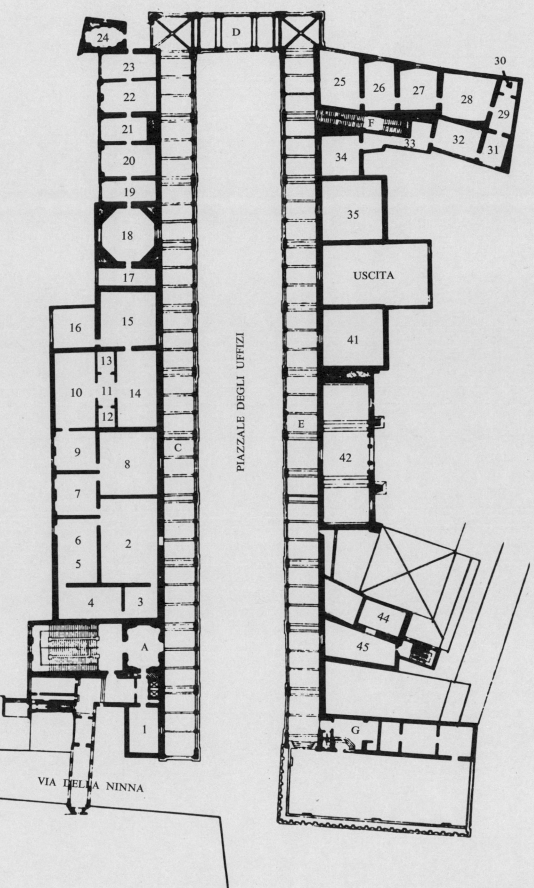

24

23

22

21

20

19

18

17

16 15

13

10 11 14

12

9 8

7

6 2

5

4 3

A

1

D

25 26 27

28

29

30

F

32 31

33

34

35

USCITA

41

E

42

44

45

G

PIAZZALE DEGLI UFFIZI

C

VIA DELLA NINNA

By kind permission of the Uffizi Gallery

SELECTED BIBLIOGRAPHY

BERENSON, BERNARD. *Italian Painters of the Renaissance* (Phaidon, London, 1953; rev. ed. 1957).

BURCKHARDT, JAKOB C. *The Civilization of the Renaissance in Italy*. tr. by S. G. C. Middlemore, 3rd rev. ed. (Phaidon, London, 1951).

CHASTELL, ANDRÉ. *The Age of Humanism, Europe 1480–1530*. (McGraw-Hill, New York, 1963).

CLARK, SIR KENNETH. *Piero della Francesca* (Phaidon, London, 1951).

CLARK, SIR KENNETH. *Leonardo da Vinci*. (Macmillan, New York, 1951).

CRONIN, VINCENT. *The Florentine Renaissance*. (Dutton, New York, 1967).

CROWE, SIR J. A., and CAVALCASELLE, G. B. *A History of Painting in Italy*. ed. L. Douglas, 6 vols. (Murray, London, 1902–1914).

DE TOLNAY, CHARLES. *Michelangelo*. 5 vols. (Princeton University Press, Princeton, N.J., 1943–60).

DEWALD, ERNEST T. *Italian Painting, 1200–1600*. (Holt, Rinehart, Winston, New York, 1961).

FISCHEL, OSKAR. *Raphael*. tr. by Bernard Rackham. 2 vols. (Kegan Paul, Trench, Trubner, London, 1948).

FREEDBERG, SYDNEY J. *Painting of the High Renaissance in Rome and Florence*. 2 vols. (Harvard University Press, Cambridge, Mass., 1961).

MC CARTHY, MARY. *The Stones of Florence*. (Harcourt, Brace, New York, 1959).

MARTINELLI, GIUSEPPE, ed. *The World of Renaissance Florence* (Putnam, New York, 1968).

PLUMB, J. H. and the editors of Horizon Magazine. *The Horizon Book of the Renaissance*. (American Heritage, New York, 1961).

POPE-HENNESSY, JOHN. *Fra Angelico*. (Phaidon, London, 1952).

POPE-HENNESSY, JOHN. *The Complete Work of Paolo Uccello*. (Phaidon, London, 1950).

POPE-HENNESSY, JOHN. *Portrait in the Renaissance*. (Princeton University Press, Princeton, N.J., 1967).

ROSSI, FILIPPO. *Art Treasures of the Uffizi and Pitti*. (Abrams, New York, 1960).

SCHEVILL, FERDINAND. *History of Florence*. (Ungar, New York, 1961).

VASARI, GIORGIO. *The Lives of the Painters, Sculptors, and Architects*. tr. by A. B. Hind, 4 vols. (Dutton, New York, 1927).

For their courtesy in furnishing information for this publication we wish to thank Emma Micheletti of the Uffizi Gallery and Gian Lorenzo Mellini of the University of Florence.

INDEX OF ILLUSTRATIONS

Page

ITALY

Pisan Cross, called *"Croce dell'Accademia"* 19
Cimabue, Madonna and Child in Majesty 20
Duccio di Buoninsegna. Madonna and Child in Majesty . . 21
Giotto di Bondone. Madonna and Child in Majesty . . . 22
Giottino. Pietà from S. Remigio. Detail 23
Simone Martini. Annunciation. Detail 25
Ambrogio Lorenzetti. Presentation in the Temple . . . 26
Pietro Lorenzetti. The Blessed Umiltà Reading 27
Lorenzo Monaco. Adoration of the Magi 28
Starnina. Thebaid 28–29
Gentile da Fabriano. Adoration of the Magi 30–31
Fra Angelico. Coronation of the Virgin 33
Paolo Uccello. Battle of San Romano 34–35
Masaccio. Madonna and Child with St. Anne 36–37
Domenico Veneziano. Madonna and Child with SS. Francis,
   John the Baptist, Zenobius and Lucy 38
Fra Filippo Lippi. Madonna and Child with Two Angels . 39
Fra Filippo Lippi. Coronation of the Virgin 40–41
Piero della Francesca. Triumphal Diptych. Battista Sforza . 42
Piero della Francesca. Triumphal Diptych. Federico II da
   Montefeltro 43
Piero dell Francesca. Triumphal Diptych. Details of the two
   Triumphs 44–45
Alessio Baldovinetti. Annunciation 47
Giovanni Bellini. Pietà 48
Giovanni Bellini. Sacred Allegory 49
Andrea Mantegna. The Madonna of the Quarry 50
Andrea Mantegna. Adoration of the Magi 51
Andrea Mantegna. The Circumcision 52
Andrea Mantegna. Portrait of Cardinal Carlo de' Medici . 53
Antonio Pollaiolo. SS. Eustace, James and Vincent . . . 54
Antonio Pollaiolo. The Labors of Hercules 55
Andrea Del Verrocchio. Baptism of Christ 56
Sandro Botticelli. Judith's Return to Bethulia 58
Sandro Botticelli. Self-Portrait (?) with Medal 58
Sandro Botticelli. St. Augustine in his Study 59
Sandro Botticelli. La Primavera (Spring) 60–63
Sandro Botticelli. Adoration of the Magi 64
Sandro Botticelli. Adoration of the Magi 64
Sandro Botticelli. Madonna of the Pomegranate 66
Sandro Botticelli. Madonna of the Magnificat 67
Sandro Botticelli. Birth of Venus 68–70
Sandro Botticelli. St. Barnabas Altarpiece 71
Sandro Botticelli. Calumny 72
Sandro Botticelli. Annunciation 73
Pietro Perugino. Madonna and Child between SS. John the
   Baptist and Sebastian 74
Pietro Perugino. Pietà 75
Pietro Perugino. Portrait of a Boy 76
Domenico Ghirlandaio. Adoration of the Magi 77
Luca Signorelli. Madonna and Child 78
Luca Signorelli. Holy Family 78
Luca Signorelli. Crucifixion with the Magdalen 79
Leonardo da Vinci. Annunciation 80–81
Leonardo da Vinci. Adoration of the Magi 82–83
Lorenzo di Credi. Venus 84
Lorenzo di Credi. Annunciation 85
Filippino Lippi. Madonna and Child with SS. John the Bap-
   tist, Victor, Bernard and Zenobius 86
Filippino Lippi. Allegory of Hate 87
Piero di Cosimo. Immaculate Conception 88
Mariotto Albertinelli. Visitation 90
Michelangelo. Holy Family 91
Giorgione. The Trial of Moses 92
Lorenzo Lotto. Madonna and Child with Saints 94
Raphael. Madonna of the Goldfinch 95

Raphael. Portrait of Leo X with Two Cardinals 97
Sebastiano del Piombo. Death of Adonis 98
Andrea del Sarto. Madonna of the Harpies 99
Andrea del Sarto. Portrait of the Artist's Stepdaughter . 100
Andrea del Sarto. St. Michael Weighing Souls 101
Titian. Portrait of a Knight of Malta 102
Titian. Portrait of Eleonora Gonzaga 103
Titian. Portrait of Bishop Ludovico Beccadelli 104
Titian. Flora 105
Titian. Venus and Cupid 106–107
Titian. Venus of Urbino 108 109
Correggio. Rest on the Flight into Egypt 110
Correggio. Adoration of the Child 112
Jacopo Pontormo. Supper at Emmaus 112
Jacopo Pontormo. Portrait of a Woman with a Basket of
   Spindles 113
Rosso Fiorentino. Moses Defending the Daughters of
   Jethro 114–115
Parmigianino. Madonna with the Long Neck 116
Parmigianino. Madonna of St. Zacharias 117
Parmigianino. Portrait of a Gentleman 118
Agnolo Bronzino. Portrait of a Youth with a Lute 119
Agnolo Bronzino. Pietà 119
Agnolo Bronzino. Portrait of Bartolommeo Panciatichi . . 120
Agnolo Bronzino. Portrait of Eleonora of Toledo and her
   Son 121
Jacopo Tintoretto. Leda and the Swan 122
Jacopo Tintoretto. Portrait of Jacopo Sansovino 123
Paolo Veronese. Annunciation 124–125
Paolo Veronese. Holy Family with Two Saints 125
Paolo Veronese. Martyrdom of St. Justina 126
Giovanni Battista Moroni. Portrait of a Knight 127
Caravaggio. Youthful Bacchus 128
Caravaggio. Sacrifice of Abraham 129
Giuseppe Maria Crespi. Massacre of the Innocents . . . 130
Giambattista Tiepolo. The Erection of the Statue of an
   Emperor 131
Francesco Guardi. Village with Canal 132

FLANDERS, GERMANY, HOLLAND, FRANCE

Rogier van der Weyden. Entombment 134
Hans Memling. Portrait of a Young Man 135
Hans Memling. The Portinari Diptych 136
Master of the Baroncelli Portraits. Baroncelli Portraits . . 136
Hugo van der Goes. Portinari Triptych 138–140
Nicolas Froment. The Lazarus Triptych 141
Gerard David. Adoration of the Magi 142
Master of the Virgo inter Virgines. Crucifixion 143
Albrecht Dürer. Adoration of the Magi 144
Albrecht Dürer. Madonna and Child 145
Albrecht Dürer. St. Philip 146
Albrecht Dürer. St. James 146
Albrecht Dürer. Portrait of the Artist's Father 147
Lucas Cranach the Elder. Adam 149
Lucas Cranach the Elder. Eve 149
Albrecht Altdorfer. Martyrdom of St. Florian 150
Albrecht Altdorfer. Departure of St. Florian 151
Hans Süss von Kulmbach. St. Peter Walking on the Waters 151
Peter Paul Rubens. Isabella Brant 152
Peter Paul Rubens. Henry IV at the Battle of Ivry . . . 153
Johann Liss. Venus at her Toilette 154
Hercules Seghers. Rocky Landscape 155
Anthony van Dyck. Jan van Montfort 156
Rembrandt van Rijn. Portrait of the Artist as a Young Man 157
Rembrandt van Rijn. Portrait of an Old Man 158
Rembrandt van Rijn. Portrait of the Artist as an Old Man . 158
Jean-Baptiste Siméon Chardin. Girl with Shuttlecock . . 160

INDEX OF NAMES

Note: Italic numbers refer to names mentioned in captions.

Alberti, Leon Battista, 46, 63, *72*, 98
Albertinelli, Mariotto, 89, *90*
Albini, Franco, 163
Allori, Alessandro, 162
Altdorfer, Albrecht, 148, *151*
Altichiero, 31
Alvarez, Juan, 54
Andrea del Sarto, *98*, 98, 99, *99*, 100, *100*, *101*, *110*, 113, *113*, 114, 119, 163
Angelico, Fra. *See* Fra Angelico.
Anonimo Magliabechiano, *90*
Apelles, 72
Aretino, Pietro, *105*
Arnolfo di Cambio, 11, 28, 166
Arslan, Edoardo, 126
Avanzi, Jacopo, 31

Bacchiacca, Il (Francesco d'Ubertino), *113*
Bachaumont, François Le Coigneux de, 159
Baglione, Giovanni, *129*
Bajardi, Elena, *116*
Baldovinetti, Alessio, 46, *46*, 54, 55
Balen, Hendrick Van, *156*
Bandini Baroncelli, Pierantonio (Piro Bonndin), 137, *137*
Bandini, Giovanni, *114*
Barberini, Maffeo, *129*
Baroncelli, Maria, 137, *140*
Bartolomeo della Porta, Fra, 89, 119
Beccadelli, Ludovico, 103, *105*
Becherucci, Luisa, 163
Bellini, Giovanni, 46, *48*, *49*, 51, *93*, 163
Bellori, Pietro, 127, *129*
Benci, Amerigo, *83*
Berenson, Bernard, *53*, 94, 108, 122, *123*
Bergognone, Il (Ambrogio da Fossano), 127
Bernardini, G., *98*
Bernardino della Ciarda, 32
Boccaccio, Giovanni, 24
Bocchi, 162
Bode, Wilhelm von, *155*
Bonasone, Giulio, *116*
Bonciani, Maria, 137, *137*
Bordone, Paris, 101
Borghini, Raffaele, *58*, *123*
Bosch, Hieronymus, 142
Botticelli, Sandro (Alessandro Filipepi), 10, 57, *57*, 58, *58*, *60*, 63, *63*, 65, *65*, 66, *66*, 67, *68*, 71, *71*, *72*, *72*, 76, 78, 87
Bouts, Dirck, 140, *141*
Braccesi, Alessandro, 76, *76*
Brant, Isabella, 152, *152*
Braunfels, 48
Bronzino, Agnolo, 118, 119, *119*, 120, *120*
Brueghel, Pieter, 139
Buontalenti, Bernardo, 11, 162, 166
Burrini, Giovanni Antonio, 129

Calmo, A., 123
Campagnola, Giulio, 93
Campin, Robert, *135*
Canaletto, Il (Giovanni Antonio Canal), 132
Cappello, Bianca, *51*, 57
Caravaggio, Il (Michelangelo Merisi), 10, 23, 127, *129*
Carletto (Carlo Caliari), 126
Carracci, Ludoviso, 129
Catena, Vincenzo, 93
Cavalcaselle, Giovanni Battista, 46, 48, 93, *93*
Cazes, Pierre-Jacques, *158*
Chardin, Jean-Baptiste Siméon, *158*, 159
Chigi, Agostino, 97
Christus, Petrus, 135, 137, *137*
Cimabue (Cenni di Pepo), 10, 18, *20*, 21, 28, 163
Ciriaco d'Ancona (Ciriaco di Filippo Pizzicolli), *135*
Colleoni, Bartolomeo, *57*
Coninxloo, Gillis Van, *155*
Contarini, Gaspare, 103

Contini-Bonacossi, Collection, 122
Cook, Collection, 148
Cornaro, Alvise, 123
Corot, Jean-Baptiste Camille, 10
Correggio (Antonio Allegri), *110*, 111, *111*, 116, 162, 163
Costa, Lorenzo, 111
Coypel, Antoine, *158*
Cranach, Lucas, the Elder, 148, *148*
Crespi, Giuseppe Maria, 129, 130, *130*
Crespi, Luigi, *130*
Creti, Donato, 130

D'Achiardi, P., *98*
Daddi, Bernardo, 24
Dante, 18, *71*
David, Gerard, 141, 142, *142*, 144
Deguileville, Guillaume, 48
Delacroix, Eugène, 10
Della Porta, Giovan Maria, 102, *103*
Della Robbia, Luca, 54
Della Rovere, family, *43*, *103*, 162
Della Rovere, Francesco Maria, *103*
Della Rovere, Guidobaldo, *108*
Della Rovere, Vittoria, 162
Desiderio da Settignano, 83
Diderot, Denis, 159
Dolfin, 132
Domenico di Francesco del Tasso, *90*
Domenico Veneziano, 38, '39, *42*, 46, 76
Doni, Agnolo, *90*
Doni, family, *90*, 93
Dossi, Dosso, 111
Duccio di Buoninsegna, 10, 18, 21, *21*, 23, 28
Dürer, Albrecht, 46, 144, *144*, 145, *145*, 146, *146*, 148, 151, 152, 163
Dussler, L., 46
Dyck, Anthony van, 155, 156, *156*

Eleonora of Toledo, 120, *120*
Empoli (Jacopo Chimenti), *113*
Ensor, James, 10
Este, Lionello d', *135*
Eyck, Jan van, 135

Facio, Bartolomeo, *135*
Fantini, Girolamo, *108*
Fede, Lucrezia del, *100*, 114
Federico II of Mantua, *97*
Federico II da Montefeltro, *43*, 44, 45, *45*, 46
Ferdinando of Tuscany, *130*
Ficino, Marsilio, *60*, 63
Filipepi, Antonio, 58
Fiocco, Giuseppe, *53*, 93, 101, 125, 126
Fra Angelico (Fra Giovanni da Fiesole), 14, 32, *32*, 41, *46*, 76
Francesco di Antonio Maringhi, 41
Francesco di Giorgio, 46
Francia (Francesco Raibolini), 111
Francis I, *80*, *82*
Francis III of Lorraine, 163
Francis of Brittany, 137
Freedberg, Sidney J., *118*
Friedländer, Walter F., *142*, 156
Froment, Nicolas, 140, 141, *141*

Gaddi, Agnolo, 29
Galilei, Galileo, 12
Geel, Jacob van, 155
Geertgen tot Sint Jans, 142, 144
Gentile da Fabriano, 31, *31*
Ghiberti, Lorenzo, 18, *32*
Ghirlandaio, Domenico (Domenico Bigordi), 76, *76*, 80, 87
Ghirlandaio, Ridolfo, 80
Giambologna, 11
Giorgione (Giorgio da Castelfranco), 93, *93*, 102, 110

Giottino, *23*, 24
Giotto, 10, 18, 21, 23, *23*, 24, 28
Giovanni da Milano, 24
Giovanni delle Bande Nere (Giovanni de' Medici), *60*
Giovanni di Zanobi del Lama, 65
Giulio Romano (Giulio Pippi), 97, 153
Goes, Hugo van der, 10, 137, *139*, *140*
Gogh, Vincent van, 158
Gonzaga, Eleonora, 102, *193*
Gonzaga, family, 53
Gonzaga, Isabella, *74*
Gozzadini, Bonifazio, *116*
Gronau, G., 46, 108
Guadagni, family, *74*
Guardi brothers, 125
Guardi, Francesco, 132, *132*
Guercino (Giovanni Francesco Barbieri), 129
Guidoriccio da Fogliano, 24

Hadeln, D. von, *123*, 124
Hartt, Frederick, 51
Henry IV, *152*, 153
Hesiod, 63
Holbein, Hans, 120
Hugford, Collection, *58*

Ingres, Jean-Auguste-Dominique, 10, 127

Jacopo de' Barbari, *151*
James of Lusitania, 54
Julius II, 99

Knapp, F., *51*
Kristellers, P. O., *51*, 53
Kulmbach, Hans Süss von, 151, *151*

Lama del, family, *65*
Lanzi, Luigi, 13, *49*, 163
Lastman, Pieter, *156*
Laurana, Luciano, 51
Leo X, 97, *97*
Leonardo da Vinci, 10, 12, 57, 65, 80, *80*, 83, *83*, 84, 87, 89, *89*, 96, 153, 163
Leopold William, *105*
Levy Morteyra, Haham Saul, *158*, 163
Liberale da Verona, 28
Lippi, Filippino, 65, 87, *87*, 89, *89*
Lippi, Fra Filippo, *39*, *40*, 41, 57, *57*
Liss, Johann, 155, *155*
Lobkowitz, Collection, 148
Longhi, Roberto, *49*, *51*, 93, *129*
Lopez, Don Alfonso, *105*
Lorenzetti, Ambrogio, 27, *27*, 28, 29
Lorenzetti, Pietro, *27*, 28
Lorenzo di Credi, 84, *84*, 140
Lorenzo di Pierfrancesco, *60*, 65, 71, 78
Lorenzo Monaco, *28*, 29, 41
Lorraine family, 163
Lotto, Lorenzo, 94, *94*, 148
Louis XIII, 153
Lucian, 72, *72*
Ludwig, G., 48, *49*
Luther, Martin, 146

Magherini, Ottavio, 67
Magnasco, Alessandro, 129
Manetti, Antonio, 54
Mantegna, Andrea, 28, 46, 49, 51, *51*, *52*, 53, *53*, 162
Manzuoli, Giorgio, *116*
Marangoni, Matteo, 127, 129, *129*, *130*
Maria del Berettaio, *100*
Marle, Raimond Van, 46
Martini, Simone, 10, 24, *24*
Mary of Burgundy, 137
Masaccio, 10, 23, 31, 36, *36*, 41

Maso di Banco, 24
Masolino da Panicale, 36, *36*
Master Guglielmo, 18
Master of Frósini, 24
Master of the Baroncelli Portraits, 137, *137*
Master of the Virgo inter Virgines, 142, *142*
Maurucci da Tolentino, Niccolo, 32
Maximilian, Emperor, 137
Mazzarino, Giulio, *122*
Mazzoni, Sebastiano, 129
Medici, Anna Maria Luisa de', 13, 163
Medici, Don Antonio de', *51, 52, 57, 83, 105, 114,* 162
Medici, Carlo de', 53, *53, 58, 94*
Medici, Cosimo I de' (Cosimo the Elder), 11, 41, 58, 65, *120,* 162, 166
Medici, Cosimo II de', *111,* 162
Medici, Cosimo III de', 163
Medici, family, 9, 32, 58, *60,* 71, 137, 162
Medici, Ferdinando de', 163
Medici, Ferdinando II de', 12, *99, 116,* 162, 163
Medici, Francesco I de', *51, 57,* 162
Medici, Don Garzia de', *120*
Medici, Giangastone de', 163
Medici, Don Giovanni de', *120*
Medici, Giuliano de', 65
Medici, Giulio de', 97
Medici, Leopoldo de', 12, *66, 89, 98, 102, 105, 124, 125, 126,* 162
Medici, Lorenzo de' (the Magnificent), 12, *51, 57, 60,* 65, 162
Medici, Maria de', 153
Medici, Piero de' (Piero the Gouty), 65
Memling, Hans, 135, *135,* 137, *137*
Memmi, Lippo, *24*
Menescardi, *131*
Metsys, Quentin, 137
Michelangelo Buonarotti, 10, 12, 90, *90,* 97, 98, 116, 162, 163
Michele di Ridolfo del Ghirlandaio (Michele Tosini), *94*
Micheletto Attendolo da Cotignola, 32
Mocenigo, Alvise, *48*
Momper, Joos de, 155
Montfort, Jan Van, 155, *156*
Morassi, Antonio, 93, 102, *131*
Morelli, Giovanni, *98,* 101, *124*
Moretto da Brescia (Alessandro Bonvicino), *98*
Moroni, Giovanni Battista, 127, *127*
Murray, John, *129*

Nardo di Cione, 24
Nasi, family, *94*
Nasi, Vincenzo, *94*
Noè Walker, Arthur de, *122*
Noort, Adam Van, *152*

Pacioli, Luca, 46
Pallucchini, Rodolfo, 102, 108, 124
Panciatichi, Bartolommeo, 119, *120*
Paolo Uccello. *See* Uccello, Paolo.
Parigi, Alfonso, 166
Parmigianino (Francesco Mazzola), 116, *116, 118, 118,* 119
Parri, Spinelli, 29
Pasinelli, Lorenzo, 130
Paul IV, *105*
Perin del Vaga (Pietro Bonaccorsi), 116
Perugino, Pietro (Pietro Vannucci), 74, *74,* 76, *76, 78,* 89, 96
Peruzzi, Baldassare, 166
Petrarch, Francesco, 24, *100*
Pico della Mirandola, Giovanni, 65
Pieralli, Collection, *58*
Piero della Francesca, 10, *42,* 44, 45, *45,* 74, *78,* 96, 162
Piero di Cosimo, 89, *89,* 90, 140
Pietro Leopoldo of Lorraine, 13, 163
Pigafetta, Filippo, 162

Pisanello, Antonio, 31, 45
Pisano, Giovanni, 28
Pittaluga, Mary, 122
Pollaiolo, Antonio (Antonio Benci), 10, 54, *54,* 55, *55,* 57, 74
Pollaiolo, Pietro, 54, 55
Politian (Poliziano, Angelo), 65
Pontormo, Jacopo (Jacopo Carucci), *100,* 113, *113,* 114, 119, *119*
Porta, Giuseppe (Salviati), 123, 124
Portinari, Antonio, 137, *140*
Portinari, Benedetto, 137, *137*
Portinari, family, 137
Portinari, Maria, 137, *140*
Portinari, Pigello, 137, *140*
Portinari, Tommaso, 137, *140*
Pucci, Lucrezia, *120*
Puligo, Domenico, *113*

Quintavalle, Carlo Arturo, *118*

Ragghiante, Carlo Ludovico, 9
Ragghianti Collobi, Licia, 144
Raphael, 10, 89, *94,* 96, *96,* 100, 105, 116, 135, 162
Rasmo, N., 48
Rembrandt van Rijn, 10, 155, *155, 156,* 158, *158,* 159, 163
Ricci, Corrado, 163
Ricci, Marco, 132
Ridolfi, Carlo, *125*
Rizzi, *131*
Robetta, Cristoforo, 57
Romanino (Girolamo da Romano), 127
Rosenberg, Jakob, 159
Rosselli, Cosimo, *89*
Rossellino, Antonio, 54
Rossi, Leone de', 97
Rosso, Fiorentino, 114, *114,* 116
Rota, Martino, *53*
Rubens, Peter Paul, 10, 152, *152,* 153, 156, 159

Sack, E., 130
Salviati, Cornelia, *74*
Salvini, Roberto, 125, 126, 139, 156
St. Anne, 36, *36,* 94, *94*
St. Anthony, *89*
St. Anthony Abbot, *140*
St. Augustine, 59, *59,* 71
St. Barbara, 125, *125*
St. Barnabas, *71*
St. Benedict, *23,* 127, *127*
St. Bernard, 87, *87*
St. Bernard degli Uberti, *101*
St. Catherine of Alexandria, *71, 89*
St. Elizabeth, 90
St. Eustace, 54, *54*
St. Florian, 148, *151*
St. Francis, *39,* 40, 99
St. James, 54, *54,* 146, *146*
St. Jerome, *78, 94,* 116
St. Job, 48
St. John the Baptist, 18, *39,* 40, 57, 71, *71,* 74, 76, *87, 101*
St. John the Evangelist, *74, 89,* 99
St. John Gualbertus, *101*
St. John, the Infant, 90, 93, 125, *125*
St. Joseph, *78,* 90, 93, 94, 125
St. Joseph of Arimathea, *74*
St. Justine, 126, *126*
St. Ignatius, *71*
St. Louis, 24
St. Lucy, *39,* 40
St. Margaret, *89, 140*
St. Martin, 24
St. Mary Magdalen, *140*
St. Michael, *71,* 100, *101*
St. Nicodemus, *74*
St. Paul, 48, 151, *151,* 152
St. Peter, *89,* 151, *151,* 152

St. Philip, 146, *146*
St. Philip Benizzi, *89*
St. Sebastian, 48, 74, *74*
St. Sixtus IV, *74*
St. Teofistz, 41
St. Thomas, *140*
St. Vincent, *54, 54*
St. Zacharias, 116, *116*
St. Zenobius, *39,* 40, *87*
St. Zeno, 51
Sandrart, G., *105*
San Remigio, *23,* 24
Sansovino, Jacopo, 122, 123, *123*
Sanvitale, 118
Savoldo, Gian Girolamo, 127
Savonarola, Gerolamo, 89, 98
Saxl, Fritz, 51
Scarpa, Carlo, 163
Schaffer, Emil, *53*
Sebastiano del Piombo (Sebastiano Luciani), 97, *98,* 119
Secco Suardo, Pietro, *127*
Seghers, Hercules, 155, *155*
Segni, Antonio, 72
Sera, Paolo del, *102, 124, 125, 126*
Sforza, Battista, *43,* 44, 45, *45*
Signorelli, Luca, 74, 78, *78*
Silva, Don Antonio, 129
Sirigatti, Rodolfo, 57
Soranzo, Jacopo, 123
Speck von Sternburg, Collection, 148
Starnina (Gherardo di Jacopo), 29, *29*
Stefano da Verona, 29
Stefano Fiorentino, 24
Strozzi, Maddelena, *90*
Strozzi, Palla, *31*
Strozzi, Zanobi, 32
Suida, Manning William, *53,* 102
Suter, *98*

Tagliaferri, Francesco, *116*
Tiepolo, Giambattista, 130, *131,* 132
Tietze-Conrat, Erica, 51, *53*
Tietze, family, 46
Tietze, Hans, 108, 122, *123*
Tino da Camaino, 29
Tintoretto, Domenico, 122
Tintoretto, Jacopo, 122, *122,* 123, *123*
Titian, 10, 101, 102, *102,* 103, *103,* 105, *105,* 108, *108,* 110, 135, 162, 163
Tolnay, Charles de, 90

Uccello, Paolo (Paolo di Dono), 32, *32*

Vaenius, Octavius, *152*
Valcanover, F., 102
Vasari, Giorgio, 11, 12, 18, 24, *36,* 49, *51,* 58, 72, 76, *78, 94,* 98, 108, *114, 116,* 118, *119, 120,* 162, 166
Venturi, Lionello, 93
Verdier, 48
Verhaecht, Tobias, *152*
Veronese (Paolo Caliari), 123, 124, *124,* 125, *125,* 126, *126*
Verrocchio, Andrea (Andrea di Cione), 57, *57,* 74, 80, 83, *84*
Vignola (Jacopo Barozzi), 166
Volpini, *40*

Warburg, Aby, 137
Weyden, Rogier van der, 135, *135*
Winkelmann, Johann Joachim, 13
Woestijne, Karel Van de, 135
Wolgemut, Michael, *144,* 152

Zanotti, Gian Pietro, *130*
Zelotti, Gian Battista, *124*
Zwarts, *158*

171

GENERAL INDEX

			Page
Introduction	. . . .	*Luisa Becherucci*	9
ITALY	. . . .	*Gigetta Dalli Regoli*	17
		Gian Lorenzo Mellini	
		Raffaele Monti	
		Anna Pallucchini	
FLANDERS, GERMANY, HOLLAND,			
FRANCE	. . . .	*Giorgio Faggin*	133
History of the Collections	. . . .		163
The Building	. . . .		166
Selected Bibliography	. . . .		168
Index of Illustrations	. . . .		169
Index of Names	. . . .		170